Dark Psychology Secret

The Secrets of Dark Psychology and the Art of Reading People. How to Control People's Minds and Use Persuasion to Influence Them

Table of Contents

contained within this document, including, but not limited to, —
errors, omissions, or inaccuracies.

Introduction

Congratulations on purchasing *Dark Psychology Secrets,* and thank you for doing so!

The following chapters will address the questions, "What exactly is *dark* psychology?" "What is the Dark Triad?" "What are some dark psychological techniques, and how can I use them to get what I want?" and "How can I guard myself and my loved ones from falling prey to dark psychology?"

There will be discussions about hypnosis, brainwashing, cults, deception, and seduction. *Dark Psychology Secrets* will explain how to recognize manipulative behavior and protect yourself against it. Non-verbal communication is discussed, which gives some hints and tips to reading people's non-verbal cues to help detect deception or manipulation. Non-verbal communication and charisma are discussed concerning attaining, developing, and maintaining healthy long-term relationships. This book will help you if your interests lie in protecting you and your family from manipulation or acquisition of some desired object or behavior—or even just out of sheer curiosity. This book will open your eyes to dark psychological tactics being used by people all around you, and you may even be surprised that you have been using some of these tactics yourself. Real-world examples are highlighted in every section—from historical events to current affairs, Adolf Hitler to John Lennon, the jailhouse to your house, there is something to interest everyone.

There are plenty of books on this subject on the market—thanks again for choosing this one! Every effort was made to ensure it is full of as much useful information as possible. Please enjoy!

Chapter 1: Dark Psychological Techniques

You may think that you have never encountered dark psychological techniques, but you would be surprised to find, or maybe you have always suspected, that in our regular day-to-day lives, we encounter people in both our personal and professional lives that use dark psychological techniques to manipulate, control, persuade, or coerce others. We may have used some of these techniques ourselves—intentionally or unknowingly. Some of these procedures are imprinted during our formative years, whereas others are learned later in life. Some psychological techniques are even used in training for certain professions—a person's ability to master these techniques helps dictate their career trajectory and degree of success in their professional life. In this day and age, not only do people practice dark psychology, but the technology we use each and every day has been programmed to utilize these techniques on us, unsuspecting users. In your very pocket right now, there is likely a technological device that is delivering the pathway to your psychological manipulation. The manipulation is so deep to the point that people will camp out overnight and wait in line for hour upon hour just to be the first to be price-gouged by the newest version of said device. It has been said numerous times that when a product is free, it means that you *are* the product. In modern times, not only are the masses manipulated by free products, but many willingly pay hard-earned money for their mental slavery. There is a multitude of methods used when practicing dark psychology. Throughout this book, we will explore some of the most prevalent or common techniques—but the list is far from exhaustive.

Love Flooding

This technique is pretty self-explanatory on the surface—showering the intended victim with positive reinforcement or flooding with love. In more innocent cases, it can take the form of an elderly relative, such as grandparents giving money and gifts to their grandchildren for good behaviors like having high grades on report cards. This tactic is similar to coerced positive reinforcement but crosses over into the technique of love flooding when the reinforcement becomes exorbitant. Other more nefarious cases involve stalkers flooding victims with unwanted attention and gifts in an attempt to develop a relationship with their victim. In this situation, the predator uses love flooding to establish a connection to the victim and tries to guilt the object of manipulation into compliance. When the flood of love is not met with the desired result, a feeling of being owed something from their victim for their abuse is used by the manipulator to justify further abuse—similar to abusive relationships where, after having physically or mentally injured the victim, the abuser showers the abused with love in the form of gifts to atone for their transgressions. This technique, whether benign, in the case of the grandparent—or malignant, as in an abusive marriage—is best used in established relationships, as it requires some level of trust between the participants. Love flooding can include bestowing not only love and affection but also praise, compliments, and gifts. Those familiar with modern and classic cinema have all watched movies where the guy gets the girl after using love flooding techniques to attract the girl's attention. Reality is that this is a fictionalized fantasy.

This practice is most often used in our personal lives, but in certain professions, it can be used, too. Bribery, overflowing of compliments, or gifts are examples of tactics of love flooding in the professional world. I spent the vast majority of my professional life working in the field of veterinary medicine, and there were many instances over the years where I was persuaded to do or purchase things that I may not have otherwise. As in most careers that have professional associations, there is a quota of continuing education that is required to maintain our licenses. Companies would exploit this knowledge and offer continuing education (C.E.) credits to allow a representative to give presentations on their product or service. Trade shows at C.E. conferences were a wealth of swag and chances to win some exciting prizes—if you give your name, business name, and email. Many of these companies, I was certain I would never pursue their product or service, but I would provide my work email and business name for the chance of a trip or spa package—or even something cool for the business.

Love Denial/Withdrawal

This technique involves the manipulator withholding something desired by the victim as a means to coerce a said victim. Love denial is often seen as the mirror opposite of love flooding but can take other forms as well. As with the method of Love flooding (and possibly to a greater extent), an established relationship is optimal for this method to work. This technique can also be used as a means to control a person that is using Love Flooding on us, often to establish a relationship with the target of said method. In this case, both parties can be using dark psychological techniques on each other, making each individual both victim and abuser. How this works is that one person desires a relationship with the other individual and uses love flooding to attract them, the object of their desire. The person who is on the receiving end of the love flooding, having recognized that they are in a position where they are desired by the predator, can then reverse the situation and use it to their advantage by using love denial/withdrawal to be further showered with gifts. This is done at great risk, as the love flooder, although potentially harmless, could also pose a great threat when denied love in this situation and may even become violent when their advances are repeatedly rejected. The love denial method of control involves taking away or withholding positive interactions such as those noted above in Love Flooding. The infamous "silent treatment" is another form of love denial. Oftentimes, love flooding and love withdrawal practices are used intermittently by the same person; although once a loving relationship has been established, the manipulator may no longer feel the need to use love flooding, the denial of love gets the desired reaction or response in the manipulated. An abusive husband or wife that "spoils" their spouse, showering them with love, attention, gifts, after having abused their partner is an example of the possible cyclical nature of these two techniques. Withdrawal of love is particularly destructive and dangerous in a parent-child relationship, although in my experience, it can be just as destructive in a spousal or partner relationship. You might have seen in recent election cycles celebrities encouraging their fans to withdraw sex from their spouses if they did not support and vote for the candidate that the celebrity was in favor of. Not surprisingly, this tactic did not work.

Love denial/withdrawal is most commonly thought of as a technique within the abusive relationships described above, but as mentioned, it can take other forms as well. An example of this is seen in a drug dealer, and drug user relationship and often is employed by pharmaceutical companies. The drug provider or dealer will give a free sample of a drug to the user, the drug may not only addict the user to the initial feeling from using the drug but may create a new problem for the user once the drug wears off. The user now must buy another dose of the drug to not only regain the feeling from using the first drug but perhaps also buy a second product to treat the condition felt when the first drug expires.

Passive-Aggressive

The technique involves using communication in an emotionally-controlled method. The aggressiveness of a statement is masked in a passive, yet contradictory, emotion such as saying something abusive in a jovial manner. In some cases, this behavior takes place in the form of an insult, and when questioned about the statement, the transgressor will play it off as a jest. An individual may resort to passive-aggressive tactics such as sarcasm to manipulate or coerce others. Persons that use passive-aggressive strategies to achieve their goal are often individuals that do not want to be regarded as overly assertive and/, or they wish to avoid direct confrontation. Sarcasm is a passive-aggressive technique in which scathing or unpleasant remarks are played off as jokes, or the manipulator may comment that they are "only teasing." In this manner, they can persuade or coerce to attain the desired response. Another modus for a passive-aggressive individual is guilt inducement. Comments are intended to guilt-trip someone into doing your bidding. In walks your partner, late without letting you know yet again, you sarcastically remark, "Did your phone die?" In this example, both of the passive-aggressive methods described are used. The manipulator desires their partner to be courteous and keep them updated (text or phone call) if their activity runs late and their arrival is to be delayed. The comment is intended by the manipulator to induce feelings of shame and guilt in the partner, and the sarcastic tone of "did your phone die?" is an indirect method to persuade the partner to alter their actions to align with the manipulators desired behavior. It is possible that the lack of a phone call was Love Denial/Withdrawal making the manipulation cyclical.

Coercive Reinforcement

This technique is similar to love flooding but in a more controlled allotment of rewards doled out as positive reinforcement for desired behavior and negative reinforcement for undesired behavior. An example of this that many of us have experienced is being rewarded for good behavior by our parent/s. This could be for a good grade on a test, doing chores, or performing in a school activity. On the other side of the hand is discipline for bad behavior such as getting a failing grade, having a messy living space, or getting in a fight at school. In two-parent households, it is not uncommon for one parent to disperse the positive reinforcement and the other parent to handle the punishment. This is colloquially known as Good Cop Bad Cop and is a famous coercive technique used by the police. In the case of the single-parent household, the lone parent is both the Good Cop and the Bad Cop. Both in the single parent and two-parent households using this technique can have negative impacts on the children. Although many times, both positive and negative reinforcement are instinctual reactions to behavior and not necessarily preconceived strategies to solicit the desired result by the parent from the child. Later in life, this same technique is used in some professions where a good job is met with an Employee of the Month plaque and possibly a raise or bonus. Conversely, a bad job can mean being demoted, loss of hours, or even unemployment. Thorndike developed a **law of effect** which states that "responses that create a typically pleasant outcome in a particular situation are more likely to occur again in a similar situation, whereas responses that produce a typically unpleasant outcome are less likely to occur again in the situation" (Thorndike, 1911). **Coercion theory** (Patterson, 1982) describes a process of mutual reinforcement during which caregivers inadvertently reinforce children's difficult behaviors, which in turn elicits caregiver negativity, and so on until the interaction is discontinued when one of the participants "wins." Coercion Reinforcement is the system by which the manipulator rewards the desired behavior and can include positive and negative reinforcement. Positive reinforcement is rewarding someone for performing the desired behavior. Negative reinforcement is defined by psychologist B.F. Skinner in his theory of operant conditioning as "the strengthening of behavior by the removal or avoidance of some aversive event." Businesses that have late fees most likely developed them as a form of negative reinforcement, enticing us to return the book or pay the bill on time to avoid a financial penalty.

Fatigue Inducement

This technique involves subjecting the victim to prolonged stress, both mental and physical, while depriving them of any relief until the desired result has been met. Instances of fatigue inducement include any behavior that intends to coerce or persuade the intended victim using tactics of repetitive actions and/or prolonged time over which the behavior is performed. Examples include a salesperson that is wearing you down to "buy what they are selling" or an interrogator (police, military) repeatedly asking the same questions and prolonging the interrogation to get compliance from their suspect. Although these methods can lead to the prosecution of guilty suspects, in extreme cases, the subject of fatigue inducement has been known to give false confessions to end the abuse. Fatigue Inducement is a method of manipulation that may be celebrated and rewarded in military and law enforcement professions. Using fatigue inducement to "get the sale" or "reel in the big fish" can result in promotions or a raise in salary for someone in sales. Some businesses offer commissions or profit-sharing; in these businesses, a salesperson may be inclined to resort to fatigue inducement to supplement their salary. Anyone that has haggled with a car dealer has likely experienced fatigue inducement. Successful interrogators are masters at fatigue inducement. Most people have at least seen a movie or TV show where the police or military officer uses fatigue inducement to persuade their suspect to submit and confess, perhaps even to something they did not do. In these fictionalized situations, the abuse serves not only as entertainment but as a means of persuasion for some, with the viewer being manipulated into accepting this behavior in the real world. Only, in the real world, the victims of this abuse are too often sentenced unjustly for crimes they did not commit and fall prey to further abuse in prison. Similarly, this technique is used in the Military on not only suspected terrorists in the form of waterboarding but on recruits in the form of boot camp. On the suspected terrorist fatigue inducement can solicit a false confession, and in the case of the recruit, it is used to reprogram the victim's identity. This technique is also used in video games wherein a great time investment is required to get a desirable item, or, with a simple financial transaction, the player can have the item instantly. At first, the player may be determined to 'grind' for the item through gameplay. But after realizing the amount of time required to obtain said item potentially exceeds hundreds if not thousands of hours of gameplay at some point, the player will give in and buy the item (or quit the game). More often than not, this fatigue inducement results in a purchase, and the profit margins of companies employing these tactics bear this out. Currently, the video game market is at a zenith in terms of profit margins, and this is a direct result of the companies using Dark Psychological Techniques on its customers: by using fatigue inducement as well as other methods listed in this chapter.

Subliminal Influence

This technique is used to manipulate the brain of the victim on a subconscious level. Subliminal Influences are cues (auditory or visual) that persuade us to think a certain way or buy a certain item. Television is packed-full of subliminal messages; from the commercials and advertisements to product-placement, our brain is constantly assaulted by these subliminal messages. Research has reported that our brains can intake visual stimuli as short as 0.003s! Subliminal messages are generally meant to "prime" our brains to the desired behavior. Growing up, my brother and I had a game wherein when we were watching a TV program or movie together, we would survey for product-placement, and the first person to exclaim "advertisement!" when product-placement is observed is the winner. It served to make me very aware of the subliminal messages of product placement in visual materials. Ironically, even though I am aware I am being manipulated, I still find myself falling prey to this tactic and purchasing a product that I may not have purchased otherwise. Media also uses this method to sway public opinion on political issues. United States ex-vice president Joe Biden credits the TV Show *Will & Grace* with swaying public opinion in favor of Gay Marriage. Once the public support was in favor of the issue, Biden's running mate Barrack Obama changed his public stance on the issue to reflect the change in public opinion that had been solicited through Subliminal Influence. To be fair, many politicians changed their public stance on this issue once it became a popular opinion. Less than ten years earlier, Gay Marriage had been voted down by one of the most liberal and progressive states in America, California. Who would have thought a television sitcom could influence Federal and State Law?

Choice Restriction

This involves leading someone to the choice the manipulator wants by only giving some of the available choices. Restaurants will sometimes use this technique to steer diners towards certain menu items and/or away from others. Reasons for this could be excess stock of a certain menu item, diminished stock of an ingredient, or the desire to sell the "special" of the day. In choice restriction, the motive of the manipulator may be to direct towards a particular choice that the manipulator wishes or away from a choice that is undesirable to them. An example of this is at food service establishments; the customer is usually limited to a certain brand of beverages. The customer has either to purchase the brand of cola offered or to go without. Originally the customer may have wanted the rival brand of cola, but unless they want a dry mouth while eating their food, they will purchase a brand that they find less desirable. This technique is often used in relationships. One half of a relationship may ask their partner if they wish to dine out but only offer a limited choice of food establishments or 'types' of food to choose from (Italian or Chinese). In a parent-child relationship, a parent wishing their child to do chores may offer the choice of dishes or laundry, limiting the choices to chores to ensure the child does some type of chore but is given the illusion of having the freedom to choose their activity. In politics, many countries have a limited amount of parties to vote for and must choose either left or right in most cases. In many countries, the two parties work together behind the scenes to maintain control while publicly passing off the illusion of choice between competing policies. In some countries, the winning party consistently defeats the losing party in rigged elections. This choice restriction not only ensures the continued control of the country but stigmatizes any dissenting opinions and ideas as all who oppose the party in power are branded as undesirables and part of the losing team. Choice restriction in politicians can not only be used to create the illusion of choice while securing the desired result but also to create conflict between two opposing sides through tribalism. This is done along the lines of religious belief systems, race, sex, and class.

Semantic Manipulation

This refers to the manipulation of a word or words such that the meaning for oneself is not the same as the victim (usually the listener) of this method of control. A manipulator can use words that are deliberately ambiguous to achieve this tactic. I think of this type of manipulation as the verbal equivalent of crossing your fingers when telling a half-truth or lie. Semantic manipulation may be the deliberate use of a word that the manipulator _knows_ the intended victim will understand in one way while meaning it differently. When interviewed in the 1990's former United States President Bill Clinton questioned the meaning of common words when asked about his affair with a subordinate. Politicians from all countries further use this technique when making vague statements about what they will do in the office once elected (or reelected). The Semantic manipulation common among politicians is evident when the only thing consistent about their position is the frequency of which it changes. This is commonly known as flip-flopping; in nearly every political debate, at least one of the participants will accuse another of flip-flopping on the uses. One such Politian was said to have changed positions on issues more frequently than they changed their undergarments. These accusations commonly occur, all while the politician who's accusing another of flip-flopping uses similar, if not the same verbiage. If a politician stays on one side of an issue long enough, they can end up on the other side of the aisle. This technique is also used by car dealers to upsell costumers on unwanted and unneeded purchases. A particular service may be given a deceptive name to manipulate the unknowing consumer into purchase a useless service that sounds important. This is how a convicted serial killer described is reported to describe language:

"Words are your words. You invented the words, and you made a dictionary, and you gave me the dictionary, and you said, 'These are what the words mean.' Well, this is what they mean to you, but to someone else, they have got a different dictionary."

— Charles Manson

Lying

This type of dark psychological technique includes not only bald-faced lies and straight-up untruths but also half-truths or the deliberate omission of information to secure the desired outcome or otherwise manipulate the victim. Everyone has experienced a situation where lying has been used to achieve some sought-after result. As a child, you may have told a seemly innocent lie about not eating a cookie before dinner or blamed another child, possibly a sibling, for starting a fight with you as you proclaimed your innocence in the matter. Most religious manuals have strong opinions against lying. In the Abrahamic religions, lying is wrong. In Christianity, the Ten Commandments define the rules to live by; to disobey any of these is a sin within the religion. The Seventh Commandment states, "Thou shall not bear false witness against thy neighbor"; put simply, do not lie. In Catholicism, the Ten Commandments are thought of as *positive divine law*; divine because they are from the Lord, positive because they are absolute with no "wiggle-room," laws.

"The Lord detests lying lips, but he delights in people who are trustworthy."

— Proverbs 12:22

Similarly, in the Jewish faith lying is wrong. Jews are taught that misleading others, even those considered heathens by the teachings of the faith, is forbidden. The Torah states:

"The remnant of Israel shall not do iniquity, nor speak lies, neither shall a deceitful tongue be found in their mouth."

— Zechariah 3:13

Muslims are taught in the Quran that lying is one of the seven greatest sins. The Quran denounces lying and even goes so far as to teach that a liar is not a believer. Hindu scripture also condemns lying and extols the virtues of the truth, stating truth triumphs over falsehood. The Fourth Precept in Buddhism condemns lies. Early Buddhists believed that the power of truth was supernatural and practiced a blessing called "the act of truth." This entailed chanting an undeniable truth, followed by what the blessing is for, believing the powerful magic of chanting the truth will bring forth the desired effect. Most Agnostics and Atheists believe that it is bad to lie. Although, there are fringe teachings by fanatics on the outskirts of all of these examples that justify lying to varying degrees in certain circumstances. Similarly, in some countries, Law enforcement is legally allowed to lie to a suspect to elicit a confession. Oftentimes, an officer of the law will tell the subject of an interrogation that their friend or a family member has told the official that the subject is guilty, and therefore it is in their best interest to confess or come clean and snitch on the guilty person (sometimes the co-defendant). This type of coercion is commonly accompanied by a promise of a lighter sentence if the subject of the interrogation cooperates, but sometimes once the Officer of the Law has what they need to convict, that promise is broken, having coerced their target with lies.

Reverse Psychology

This technique is used on subjects that are resistant to some of the other tactics listed. In this method of coercion, the manipulator convinces the victim to the desired choice or to the sought after behavior by talking up the opposite behavior or choice. Parents will sometimes resort to this practice to manipulate rebellious children to act in the way the parents want. Reverse psychology is dependent on a person's reluctance to be coerced or "bossed around." This phenomenon is called **reactance** within the field of psychology. In society, we see this happen with trends and fads of the day. When something is deemed to be bad or off-limits by adults, it becomes the cool thing to do among teenagers and young adults. Video games, movies, music, and clothing lines use this tactic, goading the older generation into rejecting their product, thus ensuring that the younger generation will perceive the product as a form of rebellion. Some alcohol and tobacco companies use skulls and death imagery to entice customers to use their products.

"I try to lie as much as I can when I'm interviewed. It's reverse psychology. I figure if you lie, they'll print the truth."

— River Phoenix (1970-1993)

As stated earlier in the chapter, this list is far from exhaustive. Brainwashing and Mind Control will be covered in later within the pages of this book.

Regardless of which dark psychological technique is used to control or manipulate, there is a directed intent. The manipulator has a specific reason, with the desired outcome in using a dark psychological tactic. This intent is the binding

28

factor in these techniques. These techniques may not always be done consciously as many times these techniques are imprinted on us at a young age. Oftentimes, these imprinted behaviors become techniques we inadvertently use on others later in life. Some of these behaviors are reinforced by different societal and cultural beliefs around the world throughout history. Even the best of us have been guilty of some version of one of the techniques listed above. We tell 'white lies,' we omit information with half-truths or no-truths. We love-flood our loved ones when we feel guilt overworking too much. Lover flooding can be used in conjunction with positive reinforcement of behaviors we wish to encourage in others in our lives. Oftentimes, these techniques can be paired together, and there is an overlap between some methods. This can be used as a means of disguising the manipulation. The "silent treatment," reverse psychology, coercive reinforcement – pick your poison, at some point in our life we are all likely to be faced with a situation that can lead to us resorting to at least one of the techniques listed if it has not happened already within our lifetime. Some societies justify these methods as acceptable when the intent is seemingly benevolent. 'White lies' are considered untruths that are told to avoid hurting another, or that are trivia. But more often than not, a lie begets a lie, and one can become consumed with keeping up the appearance of what began as an innocent enough white lie. Many of the tools for managing anger can easily become or be perceived to have become the "silent treatment."

Anger management courses recommend things such as, "Take time out," "Think before you speak," or "Go for a walk/run." Any of these actions taken too far or for too long can be perceived as the "silent treatment." Each individual will have a predetermined (but likely unconscious) idea of what too long or too far is. Using fatigue inducement is rarely seen by societal standards to be appropriate behavior. It is, however, accepted in the case of the military and encouraged within the video game industry. In the case of the military, it is seen as a necessary evil justifiable in defending the security of the nation or world. In the video game industry, fatigue inducement is rewarded behavior in the form of pay raises and bonuses for executives that milk their consumers for as much money as possible. New studies are looking into the effect some video games have on players, triggering their brain to respond in ways that encourage addictive behavior. Conversely, other games reinforce positive behavior and stimulate the brain in positive ways. Sadly, the games that use psychological triggers to induce destructive behavior are often more popular than the games that encourage positive development in the brain of the player. Game developers and companies that use Dark Psychological Techniques will increase in number as the games employing these methods continue to profit. Game developers and companies that make games that encourage positive growth and development in the brain may go out of business and disappear due to a lack of financial support among consumers. Are these game developers intentionally manipulating the players for nefarious purposes, or are they just doing their job in an attempt to pay their rent and put food on the table?

Ultimately only the individual knows their true intentions, and it is possible that we can misinterpret unintentional manipulative behavior as a person using Dark Psychological Techniques on you. Someone may use these techniques on an unconscious level due to imprinting from past abuses. The methods are still used to solicit the desired result, but the user may be unaware that their actions are manipulative. More often than not, though, those practicing these techniques do so with full knowledge and with ill intent. Sometimes, the manipulator will not only use these techniques on their intended victim but upon themselves as well to convince them that they are justified in their behavior and on the side of good. No one truly believes that they are the bad guy, although some will try to convince you that they are to elicit fear to secure power and control.

Chapter 2: Hypnosis, Manipulation, and Mind Control

Hypnosis is a technique that can be used for good or evil purposes. There are many legitimate occasions to use hypnosis with positive benefits. Hypnotherapy is used to alleviate chronic pain, lose weight, quit smoking, and to help control anxiety and depression. When hypnosis is performed by an entertainer (usually a mentalist) for an audience, it is labeled "stage hypnosis," in contrast with the therapeutic hypnosis, hypnotherapy.

There is some dispute as to what extent someone can control another person. The general consensus in psychological circles is that there is a limit to what hypnosis and mind control can induce a victim actually to do; mind control is not going to make the average person into a murderer/assassin. Most psychologists believe that there must be underlying tendencies to coerce someone into that kind of violence.

There has been much study in the covert world into mind control techniques. Intelligence agencies such as the CIA and the KGB had programs studying different protocols in the effort of maximal mind control of subjects in the years following World War II. "MK-Ultra" is an example of a program using hypnosis to manipulate and mind-control its subjects. There have been many books, movies, and TV programs written based on the idea that a super-soldier or perfect assassin can be created using hypnosis and other mind control techniques. But in reality, the results of the program were less glamorous and exciting. The subjects experimented on in the MK Ultra program underwent extreme practices that equate to torture as their minds were made into mush and rebuilt with damaging mental defects. Although MK Ultra is a program many know to have taken place by the United States Government's Central Intelligence Agency, it was experiments conducted abroad in the nation north of the border that led to the release of documents containing information on the program.

In 1979, these documents were released and detail events that have taken place in Montreal, Quebec, Canada during the 1940s and 1950s at the Allen Memorial Institute. Allen was known as a world-leading treatment center in the field of Psychiatry. The experiments were conducted on unsuspecting patients by Dr. Donald Cameron, who was a world-renowned leader in the field of Psychiatry as the head of the American and World Psychiatric Associations. Dr. Cameron was born in the United Kingdom and studied at the University of Glasgow and the University of London. Dr. Cameron was well-traveled, having practiced around the world, including, but not limited to, the United Kingdom, Switzerland, Canada, and America. Dr. Cameron was involved in evaluations of the Nazi war criminals from World War II at the Nuremberg Trial in 1945. Dr. Cameron likely learned some of the techniques he would later implement in the MK Ultra program through evaluating the Nazi War criminals and experiments on prisoners of war. Dr. Cameron would experiment on not only psychiatric patients but also his colleagues; this was a line few would cross. Usually, the victims of experiments by governments around the world are those that society considers less desirable, including persons institutionalized in prisons or psychiatric wards, or the homeless. At the time of Cameron's studies, mental health was even more stigmatized than it is today, and the victims of experimentation who came forward were treated with reactions of disbelief, if not outright hostility, by authorities. Subjects used in the MK Ultra program's experiments in Montreal at the Allen were given mind-altering drugs such as PCP, methamphetamines, barbiturates, LSD, and even insulin to the point of inducing comas. Patients were then administered with electroshock therapy 'treatments.' The term 'treatment' being used in the loosest of terms, as torture would be a more accurate description of the events taking place inside the psychiatric hospital. After hours of brainwashing to wipe the patients' slate clean, stripping them of their identity, and the cognitive ability to access the memory functions necessary to make connections inside the mind, the patient would then be subjected to extreme hypnosis techniques and experiments.

Building upon a blank chalkboard of the empty mind, the patient would be placed in a room with a tape recorder playing hypnotic and subliminal messages repeatedly for up to 16 hours in one session. These messages would be at varying auditory levels, some detectable by the naked ear, and others only heard by the subconscious mind. These would be layered in multiple indistinguishable tracks, seeming to echo like looking into a mirror through a mirror across from a mirror. This practice was called Psychic Driving; in theory, the driver can lead the patient's blank mind in any direction to achieve the desired state of being through rebuilding the subject's value system. But in practice, the subjects of such treatment become traumatized to the point of life-altering mental illness and a loss of mental and physical acumen. In later interviews with the subjects of these experiments, they reported Dr. Cameron to be perceived as almost a god among the patients and a desire to be treated by him as if it was a great honor. This is not unlike the relationship between a cult leader and his followers, as we will later expand upon in chapter four. The information on the extent of the MK Ultra program is limited. Officially the tests were ended as far as the public at large is aware. Do these types of experiments continue to this day? Many believe so, but there is no hard evidence to support what is considered to be a conspiracy theory in mainstream circles. What were the results of the program ultimately, and has any government cracked the code to create a fully controlled killing machine of flesh and blood? Over the years, information slowly trickles out, but the world may never know the whole truth about what goes on in the shadows of its governments. In today's age of information, the media uses technology as a means of mass hypnosis on the general public. The narrative on every local news channel mirrors each other as the public is programmed what to believe about the story being covered. Clear lines are drawn to create division among the viewers as taking one side on an issue paints an individual as a bad person and the other as heroic or noble. This was previously done through television and movies when the choices were limited, but with the advent of the internet, information is shared across the globe in an instant. Whereas the media of the past rallied the citizens of a nation to one common cause; in today's technological age, the power structure instead uses the media to foment division.

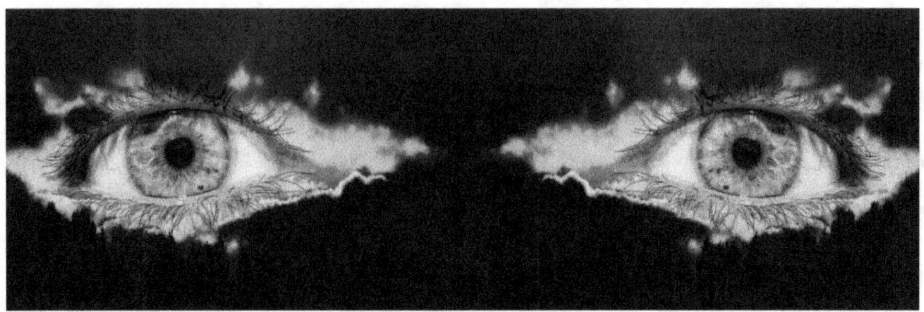

Not all hypnosis is practiced with such ill intent. Many people seek out hypnosis as a means of therapeutic treatment for a variety of issues, as was touched upon briefly earlier in this chapter. This is done during usually short sessions of an hour or two every week by a trained psychiatrist. The patient will usually lie on a couch to create a relaxed state. The psychiatrist will induce a state of calm and put the patient into a semi-conscious sleep state through the use of audio cues in the form of relaxing soft sounds and the use of a soothing voice. Once the patient is in this mental state, they are open to exploring the root of their overlying problem. Through a varying number of hypnotic sessions, the psychiatrist will dig deeper into the patient's mind and unravel the mystery of the core issue. Once this problem has been diagnosed and treated, the psychiatrist may insert positive suggestions for corrective behavior.

Hypnosis can be a form of entertainment, and lines can be easily blurred between a mental healthcare professional and a stage hypnotist (mentalist). Many times in this field, you will find claims by participants and audience members of having been treated for some addiction or other chronic medical conditions. Whether or not these audience members are authentic or plants by the performer is another question altogether. Stage Hypnotists usually have a refined charisma and stage presence, which allows them to control large crowds of people. Even those in attendance who claim to be nonbelievers have, at the very least, been manipulated to the point of separating themselves from money out of their pocket to see what they may publically denounce as a scam artist and a fraud. In a stage hypnotist performance, commonly, the mentalist will ask for willing participants. Once the participants are chosen, the hypnotist will usually use a technique known as "shocking the system"; this is to disrupt the cognitive state and put the person into a state of fear by triggering a fight or flight response. Because the participants are carefully chosen, the hypnotist has reduced the potential for fight responses and increased the likelihood of flight responses. In this case, flight equals a sleep state. This is accomplished through a strong suggestion from the hypnotist to the subject. The hypnotist will shock the subject and attempt to place the suggestion within the momentarily blank mind of the subject. This can happen in an instant when done by an expert stage hypnotist, or it may take repeated attempts. Also, it is not uncommon that a subject may not take to the suggestion at all. Once a subject is placed in a sleep state, the stage hypnotist can insert instructions into the mind of the hypnotized. The subject is given a cue, usually verbal—although sometimes visual, upon which, when triggered, the hypnotized will act in the instructed manner. Usually, this involves the subject barking like a dog or walking around like a chicken or other animal.

Many would argue that the subjects on stage are plants by the stage performer and are part of the show. This does not have to be the case as a stage hypnotist can use social pressures for people to fit in and want to be part of something bigger than themselves to elicit the needed response—and in some extreme cases, the subject is hardwired to be more susceptible than the average person to hypnosis and is legitimately hypnotized. This is why the stage hypnotist will start the show with a selection process to weed out the people in the audience that are unlikely to fall subject to hypnotism and instead select the prime subjects for mental manipulation.

Just as with the Stage Hypnotist, if you choose to experiment with any of these methods, use the utmost caution in selecting a subject and be warned that it is extremely dangerous. Experimenting on an unwilling subject is not only illegal but could result in immediate danger and possibly escalate to the form of violence on the part of the attempted subject. Many people will consider the attempt of hypnosis without consent to be a direct threat to their wellbeing and a possible sexual assault. Using hypnosis techniques such as "shocking the system" are clear examples of illegal behavior, outside of a controlled environment with consenting parties. Any unwanted physical contact is a violation in the vast majority of countries around the world and will most likely result in your arrest. If you are compelled to test out these methods at the bare minimum, get expressed written consent from the subject before attempting to hypnotize them or be prepared to face potential law action or possibly jail time. Even with expressed written consent, it is best to contact a trained professional and have them present.

Chapter 3: The Dark Triad

In the science of Psychology, there is a factor named the D Factor, which is defined as:

The general tendency to maximize one's individual utility — disregarding, accepting, or malevolently provoking disutility for others — accompanied by beliefs that serve as justifications.

In order to put that in laymen's terms, the D factor boils down to a person's propensity to be selfish, regardless of how this selfishness influences those around us, as well as how we excuse this behavior. The D factor represents all the Dark Psychological Traits, some of which can be found within each person. The diagram on the right is a pictorial representation of the D factor and describes dark traits that are included in the D factor. The Dark Triad refers to the three more nasty and vindictive traits; traits that can predict an individual's likelihood to become a criminal and can help predict recidivism. These are Psychopathy, Narcissism, and Machiavellianism. Of these three, only Machiavellianism is considered not to be pathological, that is not a disease or condition. We will discuss this component of the Dark Triad first.

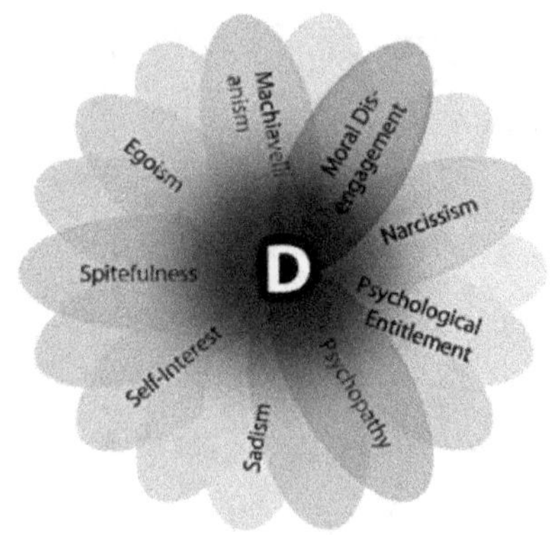

Machiavellianism

Machiavellianism is named for the espoused father of modern-day studies of political science and political philosophy Niccolò Machiavelli. Niccolò was a famous Italian Renaissance Era diplomat, philosopher, and writer. Machiavelli wrote in many genres, but his political writings are the most well-known. There are many "one-liners" attributed to Machiavelli:

"Never attempt to win by force what can be won by deception."

"Everyone sees what you appear to be; few do experience what you really are."

"He who seeks to deceive will always find someone willing to be deceived."

"Since love and fear can hardly exist together—if we must choose between them—it is far safer to be feared than loved."

"If an injury has to be done to a man, it should be so severe that his vengeance need not be feared."

"Never was anything great achieved without danger."

Psychologists believe Machiavellians not to be pathological but instead as individuals that choose to be calculating, ruthless, and cunning. Often thought of as master manipulators, these individuals are arguably among the most successful politicians, CEOs, lawyers, and others in positions of power. Psychologists sometimes refer to Machiavellians as High Machs because they score high on a test developed by Richard Christie and Florence Geis to identify these individuals called the Mach IV. High Machs have difficulty maintaining healthy long-term personal relationships and in their professional relationships, make poor colleagues but are great sparring partners. High Machs think nothing of using another person as a stepping stone, are calculating, cold, and callous. They make great conmen as they use flattery and charm to manipulate and persuade others. High Machs thrive on competition and prosper in situations or relationships with boundaries that are indistinct or hazy morally. High Machs are careful and prefer restrained tactics over blatant physical attacks. Machiavellians tend to form parasitic or opportunistic relationships.

In many of the popular TV programs, there are one or more Machiavellian characters that provide significant contributions to the intrigue in the show. In the case of shows with intrigue being a core tenet, there are often 2 or more High Machs, either in concession or in opposition, directly or indirectly. In the cross-media sensation *Game of Thrones* (Novels by George RR Martin, HBO Series for 8 Seasons) there are 2 High Machs:

- Lord Baelish, the Master of Coin for King's Landing and proprietor of a den of iniquity, has lofty ambitions and the cleverness and cunning to achieve them. Lord Baelish is a charming and poised master manipulator whose tactics coerced many a character to his will, often to the detriment of said character. Lord Baelish rarely came out on the losing end of an interaction—his sharp mind, having already thought of most of the possible outcomes, did calculate, scheme, and come up with the best tactic (and even still, he had backup plans for his backup plans).

- Lord Varys, one of the advisors to the king's court in Kings Landing, a eunuch, referred to as the Master of Whispers, with all his little birds throughout the capital, was often able to place himself strategically to his benefit. Lord Varys, also known as the Spider, weaves his webs to catch those unwary individuals he deems necessary to manipulate. Lord Varys used a possible weakness or disability (being a eunuch) as his greatest strength. His quiet, unassuming nature and the ability to be 'friends' to all from the King to a street rat or lady of the night allowed him to pass unnoticed in most companies if he wished. His network of spies kept him a step ahead of the game; with the information he possessed, he could manipulate anyone by controlling the flow of information.

When it suited them, Lords Baelish and Varys would team up, but the second their interests diverged, it was every Lord for himself.

Another modern-day fictional character that embodies the essence of a Machiavelli is the male protagonist of the TV program *House of Cards* Frank (Urquhart, United Kingdom; Underwood, United States of America). *House of Cards* was first published as a book in the United Kingdom by Michael Dobbs shortly after leaving the position of Chief of Staff to then Prime Minister of the United Kingdom Margaret Thatcher. Interestingly, the initials of the protagonist, FU, are reportedly from a doodle drawn by the author of 2 middle fingers with the letters F and U inscribed one in each, which sparked Dobbs to start writing. Drawing from his experiences in the British government, Dobbs wrote an engaging work of political fiction. The TV program depicts the political leaders of their respective country jockeying for political power, both nationally and internationally. In his journey to and in the maintenance of political power, Frank will stop at nothing. The form of writing and filming of the show gives an "insider's view" into the mind of a Machiavellian as Frank often will narrate his innermost thoughts and desires speaking directly to the audience (camera) as if he is telling you important secrets. The show follows Frank's ascent to power and the lengths he goes to get to the top. Once in power, Frank uses charm, charisma, and obfuscation to win over the hearts of the nation. Constant at his side is his wife (Elizabeth in the UK, Claire in the USA), who rivals Frank in duplicitousness and ability for treachery.

A real-life historical parallel could be drawn between the Urquhart/Underwoods and Emperor Augustus and his wife, Livia. Both marital partnerships are opportunistic symbiotic relationships that consist of 2 High Machs. Emperor Augustus was the original ruler of the Roman Empire. He used dark psychological methods of treachery, deception, and manipulation to gain power after his adopted father, Caesar, was assassinated.

In modern times the Urquhart/Underwoods are compared to the Clintons, Bill, and Hillary. Bill Clinton was President of the United States from January 1993 until leaving office in January of 2001. During his presidency, many believed his wife Hillary Clinton to be the real power in the couple and running the White House with an iron fist. Hillary famously took the lead on healthcare reform much in the same way former first lady Nancy

46

Reagan had in the 1980s with her "Just Say No!" campaign in the war on drugs. Bill Clinton used his cunning to be reelected amidst many scandals during his 1996 campaign and would even be the first president since Richard Nixon, another Machiavellian, to be impeached. Unlike Nixon, Clinton survived the Impeachment process to remain in power; Nixon stepped down in resignation before the proceeding could take place. Hillary and Bill's marriage was also thought by many to be a marriage of convenience for the sake of political power as Bill Clinton was repeatedly caught up in sex scandals with other women, and yet they remain married to this day. Whether or not this is the case, although it may be considered by many to be morally questionable, is their own business as two consenting adults. Hillary would run for political office herself once Bill finished his two terms as United States President. She won a Senate seat in New York and would run for the Democratic Presidential Nomination in 2008 against Barrack Obama, among others in an initially crowded field. Hillary and Obama were the final two candidates left heading into Super Tuesday before Obama would eventually secure the Nomination. Many experts attributed Hillary's 2008 loss not only to her lack of charisma compared to Obama but her baggage from her husband's presidency in the 1990s. Obama would go on to be elected the 45th President of the United States and offer Hillary Clinton a spot in his cabinet. Hillary Clinton would serve from 2009-2013 as Obama's Chief of Staff, overseeing Foreign Policy.

During this time, she would be responsible for many deaths, including the assassination of Muammar Gaddafi in Libya on October 20, 2011. Hillary would then famously remark, "We came, we saw, he died!" as she laughed maniacally in a televised interview. This quote was a calculated written and prepared statement calling back to the famous line attributed to Julius Caesar, *"Veni, Vidi, Vici,"* or, "We came, we saw, God conquered." Libya, under Gaddafi, was known as one of the most stable countries on the continent of Africa. Libya was a leader in women's rights among African and Middle Eastern Muslim countries. It was one of the few Muslim-practicing countries where women were allowed to vote, drive cars, and serve in the military. Gaddafi famously had an elite squad of all-female bodyguards; ironically, a woman was responsible for his death. In the wake of this event, the turmoil that ensued has resulted in the slave trade being conducted in open-air markets, as reported by USA Today. And even with this being in full public display, Hillary Clinton would run for President in 2016.

Successful political leaders are thought to develop Machiavellian qualities if they are not already predisposed to them. American President Donald Trump reportedly embodies many Machiavellian traits. His strategic mind, cunning, and ruthless behavior enabled him to be an extremely successful businessman. Some have asked the question if Trump's Machiavellian qualities caused a manipulation of the American people in electing him to office in an upset over fellow Machiavellian Hillary Clinton, or was it his Narcissistic traits.

Narcissism

Narcissus from Greek mythology is the origin of the term narcissist. Narcissists have inflated egos and feel they should be admired; Narcissus fell in love with his own image reflected back at him in the water. The *Diagnostic and Statistical Manual of Mental Disorders, Fifth Edition (DSM-5)* is used to identify individuals with a variety of mental illnesses, including Narcissistic Personality Disorder (NPD). To be diagnosed with NPD, a patient must meet five out of nine of the different criteria listed in the DSM-5. Non-pathological narcissism is a problem that has developed as a social and/or cultural phenomenon. Narcissists are drawn to careers and relationships where they can be admired and revered; their sense of grandiosity and exaggerated feelings of self-worth will not be appeased with anything less. A small degree of narcissism is arguably integral to a healthy sense of self-worth. In fact, the DSM-5 states that:

"Many highly successful individuals display personality traits that might be considered narcissistic. Only when these traits are inflexible, maladaptive, and persisting, and cause significant functional impairment or subjective distress, do they constitute narcissistic personality disorder."

Professor and author Sandy Hotchkiss originated the seven deadly sins of narcissism in her book (*Why Is It Always About You?*):

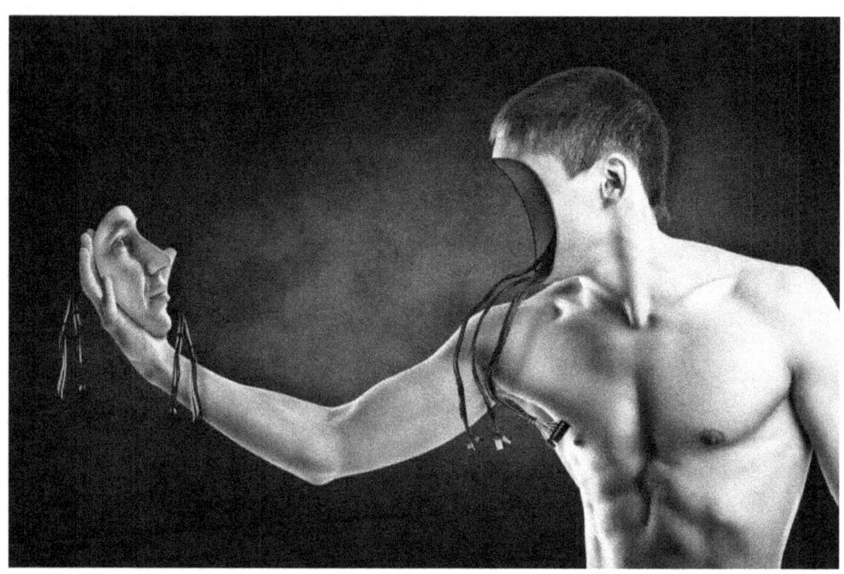

Shamelessness

This is the quality that separates clinical and non-clinical narcissists. Clinical narcissists are not equipped to deal with shame and tend to project this feeling onto others. Narcissists are never to blame; they will always try to pass the buck onto another. Non-clinical narcissists conversely exhibit a sense of shame when it is appropriate. Narcissists put themselves ahead of others at the detriment of anyone in their way and feel no remorse for harmful actions.

Sense of Entitlement

Narcissists demand attention and adoration and are offended if they are not admired for the perfect beings they are. Narcissists feel their achievements are much more important and much more difficult than others' achievements. Narcissists will downplay the achievements of others and bring the focus back to themselves. Narcissists with a sense of entitlement feel owed for their very existence by those they perceive as being blessed with their presence. This type of Narcissist wants twice as much for half off and won't be pleased with a fair deal.

Exploitative

Narcissists tend to exploit others, particularly those in a subservient role to the narcissist, and have no sense of empathy. Narcissists feel that others are there to be at their disposal. They will use and abuse others, then throw away the husks, feeling no remorse. Narcissists with exploitative traits will make their victims feel valued up until the moment they toss them to the side. These Narcissists are easily triggered to anger as they see everyone as disposable. They will appear on the surface to be very charming and may seem like a delight to be around, but the moment they do not have their massive ego soothed, they lash out at their victims.

Failure to Understand or Respect Boundaries

Others are seen as an extension of oneself in a narcissist's mind, instead of as individuals. Every time I think about a narcissist not respecting borders, I think of the romantic comedy movie "Two Weeks' Notice," starring Hugh Grant as a narcissistic lawyer and his assistant Sandra Bullock. Some of the funniest scenes are of Hugh being exploitive and not respectful of work/personal time and space. But in real life, this narcissistic trait is no joke; they will ignore your boundaries and not only fail to understand but cease even to attempt to see a perspective other than their own.

Arrogance

Narcissists feel they are superior to others, but it is often coupled with low self-esteem that they combat by putting others down with insults. Bullies are budding narcissists unless they've already become full-blown narcissists. The arrogant narcissists would reinforce their self-worth with other's failures and attribute every success to themselves even if they had nothing to do with the resulted outcome. Arrogant narcissists will direct negative attention on others to gain adoration in group settings.

Magical Thinking

The twisted thinking and illusion of a narcissist: never was there a better being than the narcissist in his own mind. In pathological narcissism, the patient is delusional. They can think they are invincible. They may think themselves a prophet, the messiah, the devil. These narcissists believe they can bend time and defy the laws of science. They are the very center of the universe itself in their own minds and believe they are responsible for every success in the world.

Envy

If confronted with a person with an ability the narcissist does not have or excel at, they are covetous but outwardly project that the ability is contemptible or may be dismissive of the ability. These narcissists hate to see others succeed and are pleased when they see people fail. When confronted by the reality of another person's success, this type of narcissist will make every effort to sabotage and destroy the object of their attention. When this narcissist brings about another person's downfall, they consider it a great success for themselves even though having accomplished nothing.

Narcissists have difficulty in maintaining the longevity of personal relationships. Their big personalities do not leave much room for someone else, let alone an equitable partnership. Narcissists lack empathy, tend to dominate when communicating, are belittling to others, are boastful, and have a tendency to blame others if things don't go right. All of these traits make the narcissists as ugly in people's eyes since they think they are beautiful.

"Narcissists are masters of pathologizing your emotions.

They convince you that your emotional reactions to their abuse are the problem rather than the abuse itself."

— Shahida Arabi

Shahida Arabi has written several self-help books on narcissism and developed a blog for survivors of abuse called Self-Care Haven. There are many self-help books, blogs, and articles available to survivors of narcissistic relationships. Many persons escaping an abusive narcissistic relationship will have symptoms like other post-traumatic stress sufferers.

Narcissism tends to appear by early adulthood, with young adults being more likely than mature persons and males showing greater occurrence over females. NPD is thought to affect about 1% of the population at some point in their lives.

The book and movie "Mommy Dearest," a biopic of Joan Crawford as a mom, as well as the experience of narcissistic abuse she perpetrated on her daughter, showcases an example of this type of abusive relationship.

It was widely reported that Donald Trump overthrew the anticipated winner of the 2016 American Presidential race

Hillary Clinton in part by "gaslighting." Gaslighting is a nefarious tactic used by narcissists to manipulate in which the victim is made to question events that occurred, their memories, and eventually even their sanity. Trump has been reported to have used Mass Social Media to gaslight the American voters. In this example, the use of the campaign slogan, "Make America Great Again," is referred to as "gaslighting" alleged by some political pundits. The slogan harkens the back to an undefined time when things were better but does not define when that was and allows each individual the ability to define the time of their choosing. Clinton used her own version of "gaslighting" during the Presidential debates. As reported by the New York Times, Hillary accused Trump of being crazy and said: "I know you live in your own reality." The New York Times trumpeted this as a victory for feminism and a historical moment as Hillary was in their reporting the first female candidate to "gaslight" a competitor during a debate. Even with the full force of the Mainstream Medias support, Hillary Clinton would still lose what was thought to be a guaranteed victory. Both Clinton and Trump were cast as the villain by the opposing side. Whether Trump or Clinton was the predator or both, it is clear that the American public was the real victim as per usual in politics. Many ascribed the choice between the two to have been that of being between bad and worse, which was, which is a question to be answered by time.

Historically, not unlike Hillary Clinton, most serial killers have a narcissistic personality disorder. Adolf Hitler is a famous narcissist, as is Jim Jones, both referred throughout this book.

Psychopathy

Psychopathy is the most malevolent of the Dark Triad. Psychopaths are bold, cruel, remorseless individuals that persist in displaying antisocial behavior. Canadian psychologist R.D. Hare developed an assessment tool to determine if an individual is afflicted with psychopathy called the Psychopathy Checklist (PCL). The checklist was developed by Hare through his work with prisoners in Vancouver and the work of Hervey M. Cleckley. Cleckley is most known for his book *The Mask of Sanity* (which provides a clinical description of psychopathy) and his work with the film *The Three Faces of Eve* about a woman with Multiple Personality Disorder. A revised version of the PCL, PCL-R, is used today to diagnose psychopathy or as a risk assessment aid to determine the likelihood of recidivism in convicts. PCL testing ideally should be done by a trained professional and include both an interview with the patient and a study of previous patient data. In practice, PCL assessment is sometimes based on case files only. The checklist contains 20 items that can be scored as 0 (does not apply), 1 (partial match), or 2 (good match) with a maximum score of 40. Individuals in the United States of America scoring 30/40 or greater meet the criteria for psychopathy; Ted Bundy, a serial killer in 1970s USA, scored 39/40. Interestingly in the United Kingdom, a score of 25/40 is the cutoff for a diagnosis of psychopathy. People with high PCL scores are more likely to be aggressive and impulsive and have a high recidivism rate. These individuals are highly manipulative and lack empathy.

The 20 criteria of the PCL-R are:

- Callous/lack empathy

- Remorseless

- Promiscuity

- Shallow affect

- Manipulative

- Many short-term marital unions

- Juvenile delinquency

- Impulsive

- Irresponsible

- Parasitic lifestyle

- Lack of realistic long-term goals

- Recidivism

- Versatile criminal behavior

- Inability to take responsibility for own actions

- Behavioral issues at an early age

- Prone to boredom if not stimulated

- A tendency to pathological lying

- Superficially charming

- Exaggerated self-worth

- Difficulty controlling behavior

Much confusion and debate are surrounding the meaning of and differences between sociopathy, psychopathy, antisocial personality disorder, and dissocial personality disorder. Not surprisingly, the famous book and movie series Psycho was about a psychopath, namely Norman Bates. This famous character sparked a TV series, The Bates Motel, that told the events leading up to "Psycho."

Real-world psycho Ed Gein was the inspiration for this fictionalized retelling of horrific events. Many horror movies have depictions inspired by the psychopathic behavior of Gein as well as biopics. Ed Gein was raised in an abusive household by an alcoholic father who died early due to complications related to his drinking and a religious zealot mother. Once Gein's father died, his mother isolated the family on their Wisconsin farm. Gein's mother would preach to the brothers, Ed and Harry, from the Bible using fear of hellfire and brimstone to scare to boys into obedience. Gein's mother preached that all women other than her were the devil. This was used to comedic effect in the Adam Sandler movie Water Boy where his mother, played by Kathy Bates of Stephen King Misery fame, exclaimed the same virtue that all women were evil beside her and that Vicki Vallencourt was the Devil. Gein would lose another family member when his brother died in what was ruled to be an accidental death at the time but later suspected to be foul play once Gein's crimes were discovered. In this instance, Gein was able to interact with the police and appear innocent enough not to warrant further inquiries. This is a common thread among serial killers as they are often questioned by the police years before being caught for their crimes. Fellow Wisconsin native Jeffery Dahmer had a similar if not crazier interaction with the police and avoided being not only arrested at the time but the police escorted Dahmer's victim back to his apartment after he had escaped even though the victim was bleeding from his buttocks and had a hole drilled into his head by Dahmer the day prior. The Green River Killer Gary Ridgeway was interviewed by the police decades before being caught about the disappearance of one of his victims and was cleared of suspicion. Ridgeway would leave his trophies from his victims in public places, including his workplace for people such as his colleagues to find. Psychopaths often keep all manner of trophies from their victims to relive their crimes. Dahmer took polaroid pictures and filled books with photos detailing every step of his crime akin to a mother keeping a scrapbook of her child's accomplishments.

These psychopaths cannot create, so they manifest their lack of success by hunting people and playing games with the authorities in a sick and twisted competition only they know is being held in an attempt to rig their own psychotic game. Just like the fictional mama boy Norman Bates, Gein took care of his mother until her death. To be a mama's boy does not in any way indicate that one is a psycho unless it becomes an unhealthy obsession. And to take care of one's mother until death is a noble act when done lovingly. It is unclear at what point he started killing and when he started to make trophies of his victims. It is also unclear the exact number of victims as Gein claims to have gained possession of his human trophies by robbing graves. Gein was obsessed with cannibalism and would steal fresh corpses from a local graveyard to do unthinkable acts upon. He would skin and tan these corpses and make masks and jewelry from their rotting flesh. He was said to have made a full outfit of his mother's skin so he could literally walk in her shoes and become her in a delusional, horrific, psychopathic fantasy. Gein claimed when interrogated by detectives that he did not remember or have control of himself when he stole the dead bodies from the graveyard. He claimed to be in a trance-like sleepwalking state and claimed to have awoken on occasion in a graveyard and left without any bodies, having become aware of his actions. Gein had a sick and perverted fascination with genitalia but claimed to have not had sex with the dead out of disgust from their smell. Regardless, there is no doubt that his actions were psychotic—and to believe his claims would be foolhardy. Never trust a psychopath!

Chapter 4: Cults and Brainwashing

There are many methods of brainwashing, each with its degree of subtlety. Some methods require the subject of the brainwashing to be unaware of the manipulation, whereas other methods require the subject to not only be aware but to submit to the manipulator freely.

Subtle brainwashing occurs in our everyday lives with great frequency. Every time we log onto the internet, we are being manipulated in subtle ways. Social media websites control interactions through timeline manipulations. Posts that will elicit a strong emotional response generate interaction. These posts can either be very positive or very negative. The more negative posts generate a greater number of interactions than even the most positive post. This is why your timeline is likely to manipulate a negative emotion from you. This, in turn, is used by advertising companies to generate sales through targeted ads. These advertisements are designed to push you to buy a product based on the emotional manipulation of your timeline. Before you have even logged on to your account, the algorithm had ads ready to display targeting the emotional response you will have to the posts in your timeline. These techniques are commonplace online in social media, and many are unaware of the psychological warfare taking part in what seems to be a mundane activity.

This is a very similar technique used by the mainstream media as present in the news. News providers decide what stories to cover and what stories to ignore. This controls the narrative and limits the flow of information. It is a subtle way that we are all victims of manipulation each and every day of our lives without giving prior consent.

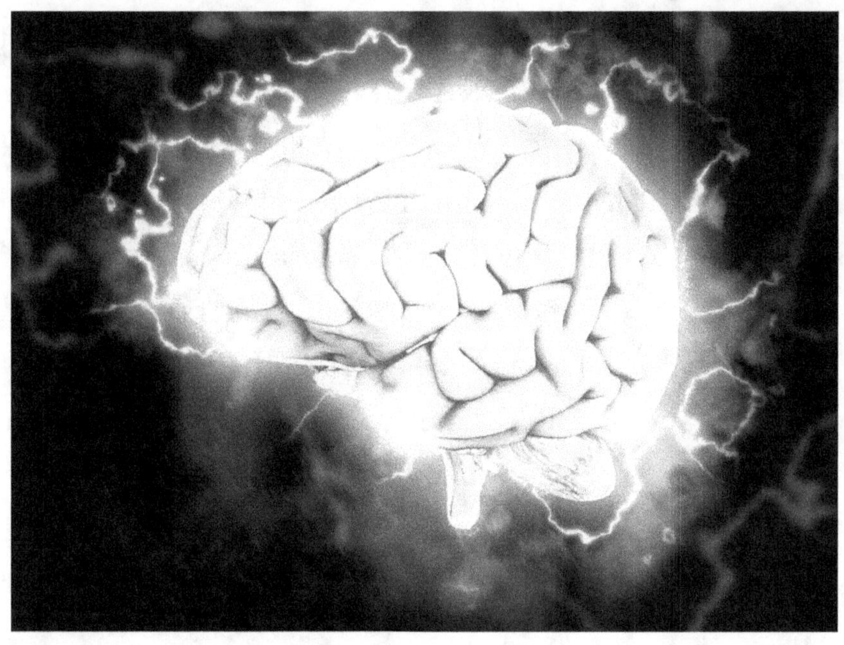

When it comes to more overt means of brainwashing, the victim gives control to the manipulation freely. This takes place in religious cults, street and prison gangs, and militaries around the world. All of these use varied yet similar tactics to brainwash their victims. In all of these examples, the predator looks for emotionally vulnerable targets to prey upon. Cults look for members with emotional voids to take advantage of. And if there is no void, one will be created through dogma and deprivation. Street and prison gangs fill a similar void in their members. These gangs provide a sense of family and community, not unlike a cult. Many of the members come from no home or broken homes. The new inmate is alone in a sea of sharks and needs to make allies quickly or fall prey to violence. In the military, recruits are subjected to extreme physical and mental deprivations in the form of boot camp. The recruit is stripped of his identity, creating a void which is then filled with the morality of his new masters. Within all of these examples, there are hard rules that must be adhered to by the members of said group. Any action that is outside of the approved behavior is met with punishment and possible exile from the group and in most cases, the threat of death. Members live in a constant state of fear that they will be shown as unworthy of the group. This enables the leader of the group to control the actions of the members.

In the case of religious cults, drugs are commonly used to render the members into a susceptible mental state, open to manipulation. Some cult leaders use psychedelics and mind-altering drugs to rewire the brains of their members. Famously, cult leader Charles Manson gave his cult members LSD to erase their former identities and recreate them in his image. Members of the cult gave witness to the events they experienced in the group while under the influence of LSD. Charles Manson would read from the Christian Bible and reenact moments from the Gospel with him playing the role of Jesus Christ. The cult members saw Manson as a God. Manson would refer to himself as a God, the Devil, and the Anti-Christ. The drugs he used on his members not only had an impact on their psyche but his as well.

Although the members of the cult were manipulated, they had freely given in to their predator. This is the case with many cults, although there are exceptions. In most First World countries, there is an age of consent; children who are brought into (or born into) cults by their parents are an example of people that had not freely given their consent to the cult manipulation. Some cult leaders use their position as leaders to create these children by procreating with the female members of their cult. In the case of David Koresh and the Branch Davidians, Koresh was sleeping with the female members of the cult and had fathered many children within the group. These children, along with other children in the group, had been given no choice. Koresh, like Manson, was reported to have given his members drugs and other mind-altering substances that were more prevalent in his time and era. Koresh used the pre-existing beliefs of his members to manipulate them. His knowledge of Christianity and his follower's already existing beliefs made it possible for him to direct their faith towards him as a modern-day prophet or the second coming of the Messiah. Building upon the structure of their religious belief system, it was not a far cry to cult fanaticism.

Another similar case is that of Jonestown. Jim Jones used similar tactics to control his congregation, manipulating existing beliefs, and then isolating his members. Drugs were also used in this case and eventually led to mass suicide. After gaining attention, the cult was investigated by the United States Government, and Jones had a Congressman killed. Knowing that serious repercussions were around the corner, once the information reached the authorities, Jim Jones laced Flavor Aid with Cyanide and gave communion for the final time. It is debatable whether or not the first to "drink the Kool-Aid" knew of the contents. But there is no doubt that the majority of the cult knew death would result from drinking the Flavor Aid after the first to drink went into convulsions and died in front of their eyes. Yet still, the control wielded by Jones over his cult members was so strong that they followed him to certain death. Over 900 people died on that terrifying day in Ghana. Mass suicide is not uncommon among cults (Heaven's Gate is another famous mass suicide (instance)) as this is but one example of people being manipulated to death.

Death as a tool of manipulation is not always the end of a victim's situation; it is, in some cases, the beginning. Street gangs notoriously require members to commit acts of violence, and even murder, to join. In this situation, the victim must freely give up control to the gang leader and follow their every order. New gang members are required to commit a crime to gain entry into the gang. This is to not only prove loyalty to the gang but is used as leverage over the new gang member. If at any point, the new gang member wants to leave the gang, not only do they fear violent retaliation from their former gang, they also face the reality of being snitched on by the gang leader to the authorities for the original crime. This puts the gang member in a state of fear and secures his place in the gang. Gang leaders also use this information to secure their gang against unwanted attention from corrupt authorities. It is a commonplace for Gang Leaders to use recruits as crash test dummies. These crash test dummies are recruits that the gang sees as expendable with no inherent value and manipulates them into crimes with the promise of entry. Instead, the Gang Leader snitches on the crash test dummy to buy favor with the authorities. Sometimes, these favors have been coerced by the authorities and traded for lesser sentences for crimes committed by members of the gang. Those that gain entry to the gang start as victims, but before long, they are part of the machine of manipulation. Once a new gang member has committed their first murder by order of the leader, they must now be branded. The new gang member is given a teardrop tattoo under their eye to represent that they have done the dirty deed. The tattoo is a permanent mark representing a lifelong dedication to the gang. The new gang member is also branded literally in many cases with the gang name or initials. This physical branding, both the brand and the tattoo, reinforce the control of the gang and its leader over the victim. These are extreme manipulation tactics of violence, both physical and psychological, over the victim. The new gang member now acts as a living breathing billboard for the gang. The gang member creates fear in their local community with their very presence and reinforces the community's fear of the gang. The gang and its leader not only manipulate and control the gang members but the community at large.

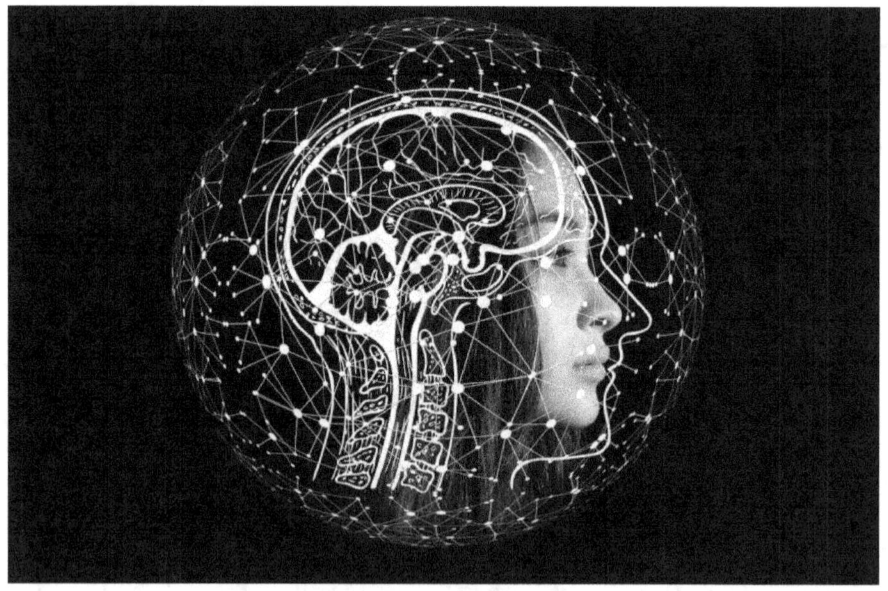

Communities can not only be victimized by cult-like manipulation but can be a force of influence upon its members; this is the case with the Military. Recruits are often attracted to serve out of a sense of duty to their community. In some countries, service is not a choice but a requirement. Even in countries where service currently is not mandatory but on a volunteer basis, service was a requirement in the not too distant past. Failure to serve in the Military can result in imprisonment in countries that require service by law. Once a recruit joins the Military, whether by choice or by force, the recruit is subjected to extreme manipulation by way of boot camp. Boot camp is the initial training for recruits and serves as a method of brainwashing. Recruits are subjected to extreme sleep deprivation, nutrient deprivation, and fatigue. Depriving the recruits in these ways renders the recruit into a mental state where their minds become putty to be molded like clay by their Drill Sargent. The Drill Sargent verbally abuses the recruits while they perform acts of physical exertion after having been deprived of sleep and proper nutrients. This leads to extreme mental and physical fatigue. While in this state, the Drill Sargent strips bare the psyche of the recruit until they are nothing. Once the recruit has been expunged of their pre-existing identity, the Drill Sargent builds them back up with the morality and beliefs of the Military. The recruit is rewarded for good behavior, in the form of compliance, with sleep and nourishment. The recruit, through manipulation, is taught to be a state-sanctioned killer.

Once full conformity has been achieved the recruit will kill the enemies of the state upon the request of his superiors; not unlike the cult brain of the gang member following orders from the gang leader to kill, or the cult member following orders from the cult leader to kill themselves or others in extreme circumstances.

What attracts many into these situations is the predilection to be controlled, or, the "Cult Brain." The Cult Brain is a state of being where one gives up autonomy to a leader. The Cult Brain is an attractive state of being for members of cults and the like. Members of these groups report a feeling a blissful ignorance and relief of stress in giving up all control to a leader who makes their decisions for them. People that have reached a breaking point in their life become attracted to this mental state as a means to eliminate the stress of their day-to-day. Many cults recruit their members from among the homeless and destitute. But conversely, religious cults also attract wealthy members that are looking for the same relief. Once indoctrinated into the cult's belief system, the Cult Brain takes over. The Cult Brain gives all decision making over to the group and the leader, and not only follows orders but rationalizes the illogical requests of the cult leader. The cult leader is the center of the universe for those in this mental state. Everything is justified no matter how absurd it may seem at first glance as the cult brain seeks only to serve and protect the leader of the group. The cult leader is God to the followers of the cult and, therefore, can do no wrong in the eyes of the cult brain. The cult leader takes care of every problem and is always the solution. Many cults reinforce this way of thinking by providing members with a communal living space and serving communal meals to the group. By taking care of the basic necessities of the cult, the leader manipulates the members into a false sense of security. This security allows the members to rationalize the loss of freedom in other day-to-day activities. The cult brain believes that the leader takes care of them and controls not only the cult but the entirety of existence. Any attempt by an outsider to logically reason with the cult member is seen as heresy. Outsiders to the group are labeled as liars and enemies. This creates a situation of us versus them and reinforces the tribal instincts of all humans that date back to the beginning of time. By concentrating energy towards an enemy, it focuses the group on one common goal and solidifies the control of the leader over the members of the cult. By creating an enemy, a sense of fear is established within the group. This fear further secures the leader's omnipotence among the group, as only the leader can save them from this enemy, real or imagined. The group is also brought closer together in the sense of sameness and familiarity juxtaposed against the external threat of the created enemy. Because the leader is seen in the eyes of the cult brain as a God, all actions are justified, even if on the surface, the actions contradict even the belief system of the cult.

Though some may have an inherent attraction and predisposition to fall prey to cults due to a pre-existing mental state, others are transformed psychologically into the state of the Cult Brain. This occurs through recruitment by the cult of vulnerable individuals. Cults and cult-like groups look for people that are going through trauma in their lives. These cults prey on the weakened mental state of their victims. Recruiters of these groups look for typically young adults that are out on their own for the first time. Many cults recruit on college campuses and use issues of the day to attract new members. Upon first glance, the recruit may think that the group is just trying to make the world a better place and that nothing irregular is transpiring. These cults blend in with other student groups and seem normal to the outside observer. It is only once the vulnerable member has been rewired into the cult brain that the true agenda of the cult is revealed. At this time, the brainwashing takes over and justifies all abnormal behavior of the leader and the group. Many times recruiters will befriend vulnerable individuals and slowly over months steer the victim in the direction of the cult. After a level of trust has been built between the recruiter and the potential new member, only then will the recruit be brought into the fold and given the final push to join. Similar tactics are used by salespeople to close deals. Isolated individuals are particularly susceptible to this manipulation. If not already isolated, the cult will urge the new member to isolate themselves from their family and any outsiders of the group. This is done to control the narrative and the flow of information among the cult. The goal of the cult leader is to completely envelop the cult members within the reality created by the said leader. Every waking moment any and all energies are given to the cult in servitude. Every aspect of the member's life is encapsulated by the cult, leaving them no room even to contemplate an alternative existence outside of the group.

Chapter 5: Dark Psychological Seduction

For one to seduce another with dark psychology, charisma is the cornerstone of building a successful seduction. People that possess charisma are magnetic and enthralling. Charismatic people have an undeniable presence that captivates those around them, drawing them in and making people hang on their every word.

Some charismatic people are born, but fear not—we can all increase our charisma through training, hard work, and diligence. Developing charisma can be a priceless tool for helping all interpersonal interactions. A charismatic person is not only a good speaker but also a good listener. Cultivating and employing good non-verbal communication skills will improve your charisma. Persons with charisma make those around them feel comfortable. The charismatic individual is confident and relaxed and can highlight our own strengths. They make every individual feel important and heard. An example of this would be to say that you, the reader, made a good decision in buying and reading this book. Your purchase is proof of your high intellect. The fact that you have made it this far into the book and can comprehend the subject matter written therein proves that you are smarter than the average person on earth. Believe it or not, but this is a factual statement, yet it could be used to manipulate and seduce in the same way many celebrities and political leaders have used throughout history. It is easy to see why many famous and infamous leaders have been highly charismatic.

Arguably one of the most charismatic leaders of the 20th century was Adolf Hitler. The correlation some people have drawn between the Nazi leader and charisma has given a negative perception of this characteristic. Adolf Hitler was able to use his charisma to seduce and manipulate an entire nation using dark psychological techniques. He preyed upon a vulnerable nation and used many of the methods described earlier in this book to gain power and control. Many forget, if they even knew in the first place, that Adolf Hitler was democratically elected to public office. Through false flag terrorist attacks on his own nation, he further secured his power to become a dictator with overwhelming support among the populace. When listening to his speeches, one cannot deny the strong emotions expressed in the tone and inflection of Hitler's verbal communication, even without understanding his language. A sense of dread and fear can overcome students listening to the recordings of this madman's calculated manipulations nearly a century later. This was not the feeling in the 1930s and 1940s Germany among his supporters. Those listening to his speeches at this time took on the personality and the thought process of the speaker. Hitler preyed upon their already existing fears and offered the listener an enemy to focus their manufactured anger towards. Germany after World War I was war-torn and filled with poor and starving people. These people feared for their daily survival and were in search of answers. Hitler would give them the answer in the form of hate directed at an external enemy, which he preached has infiltrated the community and nation at large. The seduction of a large group such as a community or a nation often requires an outside threat to the survival and way of life of the group. These threats are used by charismatic leaders to rally the troops and the nation as a whole in common cause to fight against a perceived evil, whether real or manufactured. Sadly, in politics, we see some of these same tactics used again and again over the years throughout history and in the current day. Rahm Emanuel, former mayor of Chicago, former United States Congressman, former Clinton cabinet member, and Obama's Chief of Staff for 2009-2010, famously said on television during an interview that "a good politician never lets a tragedy go to waste."

Barrack Obama is one of the most charismatic leaders of the 21st century and, during the 2008 election cycle, a prime example of a cult personality. Obama rose to prominence from near obscurity when he was given a spotlight to speak at the 2004 democratic national convention. The Democratic nominee John Kerry would go on to lose the election to incumbent George W. Bush later in the year, but on that night in Boston, Massachusetts, a national star was born in the world of politics. Obama would transcend politics with his popularity and even borders as he not only campaigned in the United States but around the world. Obama was met with huge crowds everywhere he traveled and was showered with praise among all nations of the world and its leaders. This was in a time when the current President of the United States, George W. Bush, was openly spurned and rejected by world leaders. He was even attacked during a press conference by a reporter from a foreign nation. Barrack Obama won the election over John McCain, a new President was assured either way due to term limits, but McCain was seen as the old guard and Obama represented change and hope. The victory of Obama was celebrated in the streets of Chicago, Illinois, Obama's former base of operations, as people joyously expressed what can only be described as euphoria on national television for the entire world to witness. The scene was akin to that of a religious gathering at an evangelical church as the attendants praised and worshipped the 45th President-Elect on that cold November night in 2008. One cable news opinion host exclaimed earlier in the election cycle that he had a tingling electric feeling of thrill running up and down his leg when he heard Obama speak. Obama made everyone who supported him feel like they were the good guy and that as long as he won, everything was going to be alright. This came on the heels of an economic recession and what was the largest government bailout of the bank in history. The media had inundated the public with feelings of dread and despair over their future. The whole of society was said to be on the verge of collapse unless the politicians robbed the taxpayers of trillions of dollars and handed all over to Wall Street and the Big Banks, who had created the financial collapse in the first place. A country held at figurative gunpoint was extorted once more as the rich got richer while lining their pockets with the hard-earned money of the blue-collar working man and the shrinking middle class. After this theft, the country desperately looked for a leader who would take them out of the darkness and despair. Enter a leader who promises Hope and Change. The feeling of euphoria from Obama's November election victory celebration was short-lived.

As soon as President-Elect Barrack Obama started to announce his cabinet members, it was clear as day that Hope and Change were, in reality, just more of the same. Obama gave positions to Wall Street and Big Bank representatives while imprisoning a record number of African Americans for non-violent crimes and drug offenses. His worldwide popularity earned him a noble peace prize while he expanded the number of United States troops deployed in two different foreign wars. Even though clearly abandoning his campaign promises of 2008, such as closing down Guantanamo Bay, Obama easily won reelection in 2012 over Mitt Romney. A little known fact is that Barrack Obama is related to former Presidents Harry Truman, George W. Bush, and Bush's Vice President Dick Cheney. Every United States President before Donald Trump is/was related to the Queen of England coincidentally.

Interestingly, internet polls asking who the most charismatic people of all time have quite a diverse cross-section of individuals. Along with Hitler mentioned earlier, Jesus Christ, Madonna, and Queen Elizabeth are among the most voted for in these polls. Developing charisma may be an arduous undertaking for some people; nearly everyone can make themselves more charismatic. When training your charismatic self, you should have realistic expectations; not everyone can be Winston Churchill or John Lennon. Charismatic individuals exude confidence, even when they are feeling nervous or uncertain. By mimicking the facial expressions/gestures, posture, and bodily gestures, we can feign confidence (fake it 'til you make it). True confidence is cultivated through self-love or self-esteem. A strong love of self is an integral part of achieving and maintaining a romantic relationship.

How to Improve Self-Esteem

There is a plethora of information out there focused on improving self-esteem. There are websites, blogs, seminars, courses, and the like, all to improve self-esteem. Many, if not all, focus on self-love and how to improve your feelings of self-worth. Similar tenets exist for many of these self-help how-tos for improving self-esteem.

Be Mindful of Negativity

Negative thoughts and negative stimuli cause us to feel and express negativity. Feeding into our own negativity is akin to a domino effect where one negative thought leads to another and another until you are in a deep depression. Not only can this create a repetitive cycle, but it can also attract outside forces to engage with you and make a bad situation in life even worse. Predators look for targets that are vulnerable and can spot a person going through a depressive episode in their life, as explored earlier in this book, notably chapter 4. Being mindful of your negative feeling is the first step in defending against such predators. Once you are aware of the negative thought process, you can use different methods to fight off negativity.

One such method is to replace negative thoughts with positive thoughts. It sounds easy enough on the surface, but it can be a lifelong battle that must be fought daily. Even on the best of days, it is not unnatural for a person to have a negative thought or feeling. It is the reaction to the feeling that can make the difference. By letting the negativity take control of your present state of being, you are choosing to stay in that emotion. It can be very difficult, but if you decide to concentrate your energy on positive things, then you can change your mood, even if you cannot change the situation. In Alcoholics Anonymous (AA), there is a prayer that opens every meeting called the Serenity Prayer, "Please grant me the serenity to accept the things I cannot change, the courage to change the things I can, and the wisdom to know the difference." Whether or not you believe in a higher power, the core value within this prayer can be a valuable tool to overcome depression brought on by negativity. If something is bringing about negative thoughts and feelings, and you cannot do anything about it, stressing the situation and giving in to these negative feelings will only make matters worse. It is better to concentrate on the matters at hand that you can do something about and put your energy into that area of your life to make a positive change for the betterment of yourself and build up your confidence, self-esteem, and self-worth.

Forgive Yourself

Unless time travel becomes available, we can't change shameful or regrettable actions of our past. You need to cut yourself some slack, forgive yourself, and learn from your past errors. This also harkens back to the Serenity Prayer and may sound cheesy, but holding onto guilt leads to self-doubt and destroys confidence. Hating yourself for your mistakes does not teach one the lessons needed to be learned from the wealth of experience each and every one of us has within our lives. Turn your negatives into positives by using them as learning experiences and bless yourself with the gift of forgiveness. It is not only healthy to forgive yourself but to forgive your transgressors as well. Holding onto a grudge, whether against yourself or your enemy, is detrimental to your health and overall well-being. To err is human but to forgive is divine.

Champion Yourself

Each and every one of us is good at something. Each person has their own strengths and weaknesses; each individual has some talent. It can seem as though you may have nothing to champion yourself over, and the thought of it may also seem boastful, but it is a key to unlocking your inner confidence. If you do not know what your talent is, it is not for lack of talent but a lack of recognition. If you let negative feelings and thoughts cloud your thought process, it can be hard to see your own talents amidst the fog. It can be helpful to ask people in your life—such as a friend, family member, teacher, or coworker—what they may think you are talented at. Do not distress if those around you do not recognize your talents either. Some of the most talented people throughout history were not recognized among their community until going out into the world and being discovered as having talent, only to return and be celebrated as a conquering hero. In the Gospel of Luke, it says, "A prophet is never accepted in his own country." If you don't champion yourself, no one else will. But once you do, you may be surprised at how your confidence attracts others to recognize your talents. A world-famous example of this is Muhammad Ali, known to be one of, if not the, greatest boxer in the history of the sport. The reason why Ali was so famous and popular is that he championed himself and exuded confidence and charisma. He told the world he was the best, and the majority of the people believed him. Never mind that he lost plenty of boxing matches, and other boxers had better records. When it came to championing himself, he was the all-time greatest.

Change Your Own Narrative

This is similar to being mindful of negativity and is in direct tandem (harmony). You need to redirect your story by thinking positive. Scientific studies show that positive perceptions correlate with positive outcomes. Instead of approaching a situation with a defeatist attitude, one must channel their energy in a positive direction to accomplish goals in life. Instead of saying, "No, I can't do it," say, "Yes, I can." If you tell yourself that you can do something enough times, you will start to believe it. Once you believe in yourself, you will have the confidence to overcome previous obstacles keeping you from achieving your triumphs and victories in life. This does not mean you will not have failures along the way, but through perseverance, success will be possible. Every success story starts with tales of failure before rewriting the narrative into what from the outside seems to be a given. If—in the face of these defeats—one was to quit and give up, none of the greatest feats of our time would have been possible. There is no such thing as an overnight success. Every comic does 'bomb' their first set and hears plenty of boos and jeers before the sweet sound of laughter fills the room, signifying a turning point on the road to success. This starts with believing in yourself and then reinforcing the positive energy, seducing one's self with self-love creating a narrative where your dreams come true. If you tell yourself that this does not work, then you have already defeated yourself. But if you tell yourself that it does work, you have nothing to lose but a few daydreams. All of the greatest accomplishments of mankind started with one person believing that they could do what was thought to be impossible by the masses and society at large—one person dreaming the impossible dream and achieving the impossible goal.

Avoid Comparing Yourself to Others

You have your own skills and abilities, and they have their own talents. You may be strong in areas that the other individual is weak. There are ways to bolster areas where you are weak, but comparing yourself to someone else is futile and leads to envy, which is a notorious killer of self-confidence. Not only that, but envy is an unattractive quality and will tend to repel rather than appeal to others. Seduction is not a competition between you and someone else. Seduction is about making yourself the most attractive you that you can be. Comparing yourself to others is a waste of your time and energy and only serves to stray you away from accomplishing your goals.

Seduction is naturally thought of as being a sexual conquest, but this is far from the only use of this Dark Psychological Technique. In Chapter 8, we will explore the 10 emotional types of manipulators, and one of these is "The Flirt." The Flirt uses seduction to get all things in their life. In the case of the Flirt, an over-use of sexuality is used to seduce their victims, but this does not mean that seduction cannot be used in subtler forms to achieve a goal.

Stoplights in Seduction

Non-verbal (and verbal) communication is one of the keys to having good charisma when practicing the art of seduction. Working on these skills explored in more detail, later in chapter 7, will help you become more charismatic. Being able to read and assess nonvisual cues is essential for seducing a partner. Watching the posture and mirroring it if able, watch facial reactions on the other individual to evaluate the interaction and decide whether the stoplight is green, yellow, or red. If the light is green, proceed with the interaction, maintaining the status quo, and possibly move ahead (metaphorically and physically) within the interaction. Yellow light should caution you the interaction is lukewarm. You may need to ease back a bit and re-evaluate the situation, or cautiously maintain the status quo. Red means stop. Take a step back, reassess. If the other individual seems willing and comfortable, you could cautiously probe the reason the interaction's getting a red light. Always be ready to quit the interaction if the red light either continues or reappears.

The Green Light

This signals that it is okay to proceed. The other individual demonstrates: Open body language (leaning in, arms not crossed, engaged in the communication); Maintained eye contact, or perhaps with brief glances away and sidelong glances in a flirty coquettish way (pupils may be dilated); Physically moving closer, perhaps even touching; These are all good signs that your advances are being met in a receptive and positive manner. This is not a full-proof guarantee that the subject of your seduction is aware of your intentions or that they desire you to take it to the next level. They may be just being polite and/or following cultural costumes. It is, however, safe to further test the waters unless given an indication otherwise.

The Yellow Light

Slow down and be prepared to stop. The other individual demonstrates removal of open body language (if previously had a green light) or neutral body language (upright posture, perhaps less engaged in the communication; little or no eye contact (looking around, on their phones); physical distance is likely similar to interactions with acquaintances. If the physical proximity increases, do not close the gap. The subject of your attempted seduction may be looking for a way out of the interaction, and you are best to back off. Even if they are open to your advances and trying to get you to "chase them," it will only serve to reverse the power dynamic, at which point you may end up in a love denial/withdrawal relationship as explored in chapter 1 of this book. If your advance is being spurned and you chase after someone attempting to create space, it very well may end up in a red light or, even worse, a restraining order.

The Red Light

Cease and desist immediately. Failure to do so can not only result in legal troubles, such as fines and even jail time—but in many countries, you may become branded a social outcast, and the stigma can follow you for the rest of your life. A red light is when the other individual demonstrates verbal commands, closed body language, avoiding eye contact, or physically moving as far away as possible within the situation.

The last thing you want to do when attempting to seduce another is to choose the wrong subject. Just like a Stage Hypnotist attempting to hypnotize when attempting to seduce, you must direct your efforts at a willing subject. Any attempt otherwise is doomed to failure or worse.

Seduction as a Tool

The word seduction originates from Latin, *seducere,* which means to draw to the side. It can be used in a negative way to imply decisions made while under the influence of the seducer that would normally not occur. Seduction can refer to the process of coercing a person in a current relationship astray. In a more positive light, seduction can refer to benign attempts to approach and charm another person. As we have seen previously in this book, the good or bad (evil) of using Dark Psychological techniques is dependent on not only the intent of the individual but the result of the actions taken. The road to hell is paved with good intentions. You may have the very best of intentions, but if the result of your actions leads to harm, it can turn good intentions into rationalizing evil behavior.

Is using Dark Psychological Secrets and techniques to seduce inherently evil? The simple and short answer is, no, it is not. Does this mean that these techniques are more commonly used for good? Hardly, but to answer the question of how to determine whether or not an action is evil is a deep philosophical question upon which an entire book could be written and still not scratch the surface of the question or come to a conclusive answer. Every culture has a varying degree of judgment on what is considered good and evil, although most moral standards have many overlapping beliefs. Seducing someone to take advantage of them in any way is considered immoral in nearly all cultures. Contrastingly, to seduce someone to the end of building a mutually loving relationship is considered in most cultures to be a moral good. If the intent of the seduction is to lure someone from a marriage, it was considered historically to be evil, but in modern times, some cultures find it socially acceptable, although a grey area. Whether or not the seduction is evil can be a matter of perception, depending on the bias of who is giving their opinion. A parent who has arranged a marriage for their child may see an outside seducer as being evil and having committed a great transgression against them. But in the eyes of the seduced, it can be seen as being saved from a situation, not of their choosing.

Seduction is a tool used by both males and females, both in the opposite sex or same-sex pairings. Stereotypically, males are found to be more masculine and females more feminine, but this is not always the case. Some seduction techniques will work better on more masculine individuals rather than feminine individuals whether or not they adhere to social stereotypes. There are general rules of thumb, but just as each individual is different, so must each approach at seduction be different. This means that there is no one full-proof method to guarantee success in seduction. One must be fluid and open to taking in information to gain an understanding of the correct path to follow forward. If you are not able to find a successful approach, it is likely not a flaw in your appraisal of which technique to employ. Instead, it is likely an unwillingness to recognize the subject as not being receptive to your seduction. At this point, it is best to cut your losses, stop wasting your time, and spend your time and energy on someone open to your seduction and encourages engagement.

Steps to Seduction

Most techniques of seduction involve some level of manipulation. Several of the Dark Psychological Techniques can be used to assist in seducing someone.

Here are the steps to seduction:

First Step: Identifying Interested Participants

First, you must determine the level of interest from your potential subject of seduction. Interested participants in seduction will engage and be receptive to your advances. The choice of subject is the single most important factor in the success of the seduction. If you choose the wrong person for an attempt at seduction, failure is all but a guaranteed outcome. Nothing is impossible, but a bad choice at the start of seduction will lead to a loss of time, energy, and resources that would be better spent on someone else. The time wasted on a difficult or failed seduction can lead to missed opportunities for success with someone else. If you are trying to use seduction as a means to making a sale, a bad choice in time management going after a denial of service can take up the time in which you could have made multiple sales. You have to know where to pick your battles and which are worth fighting for. An important perspective to have in determining the subject of your seduction is to have an abundance mentality. Know that there are plenty of people in the world for you to choose from for seduction. Do not have a famine mentality. This leads to bad decision making and encourages you to waste your time in an attempt to chase after a failure instead of pursuing success. It is possible to misinterpret a subject either way, but it is better to err on the side of caution. Few opportunities will be missed because of misreading a subject as unwilling compared to the time wasted chasing after them. A misread on the opposite side of the spectrum can be remedied quickly as long as you cut your losses at the first sign of a Red Light.

Second Step: The Approach

Once you have identified the subject of your seduction, you need to determine the correct approach moving forward. Each individual is unique, and what works with one person may fail with another. The key to choosing the correct approach is gathering information. You must be a good observer of your subject's behavior. This includes how they carry themselves in social settings and what type of standards and morality they hold. Opposites can attract and sometimes a moral belief in your subject may be an indicator of when to mirror and when to oppose their morality. Just agreeing with someone does not automatically endear oneself to their subject. It can instead lead to rejection if overdone. A subtle mix of agreeing and disagreeing on opinions and ideas can be attractive to some but always lean towards being more agreeable than confrontational. All for the better if these agreements and disagreement are genuine. People can sense when you are blowing smoke up their ass and do not appreciate being deceived. No one likes a jellyfish without a spine whose opinions change with the wind, although many politicians are successful in seducing voters with this approach. Regardless of the approach, being confident is key and will assist you in being charismatic. If possible, it is best to enter the engagement of the subject with a well throughout the approach and use your first interaction to make a good impression. Ways of doing this include simple things like being well-groomed. Not all of us have the same budget to work with but do the best with what you have to work with; people will appreciate the effort put forth. But don't go too far and try too hard. Some people like assertiveness, but others may find it off-putting. Finding balance in your approach is the key here. When speaking to someone for the first time, it is always good if you can make them laugh. The ability to make others laugh is one of the most attractive qualities a person can have. Again you don't want to overdo it and try too hard because an attempt at humor can easily cross over the line into making-fun-of and being perceived as a bully. In some cases, that may be seen as attractive, but it is best not to pursue individuals of this nature. Keeping things light-hearted is generally the best approach. People at their core want to have a good time, and if you are seen as someone they can have fun with, this will be an attractive quality.

Third Step: Develop Trust

At this point in your seduction, you have already identified your subject and determined an approach; in other words, you have an in. Your subject is open to your seduction, but this does not mean your ultimate success is a given. A misstep at this stage of the seduction can lead to failure. The only way to truly develop trust is through honesty. Any lie discovered by the person you are seducing will lead them to distrust you and most likely end the relationship or put it into a state of purgatory. It is ill-advised to be dishonest with your subject of seduction, but if it is unavoidable, you would be best served to cut your losses here and find a new subject. You may get away with your lie for a time, but the longer it takes the subject to discover your dishonesty, the potential for greater destruction in your life. Developing trust involves spending increased time with your subject. In the case of a romantic seduction, this can be in the form of a date or agreeing to meet up in a social setting to enjoy each other's company without labeling it. In the case of setting up a business relationship with the goal of the seduction being an eventual sale, one may invite their subject to a recreational event or activity. This could be going out for appetizers and drinks, playing a round of golf or squash, going out to a sporting event, or local social gathering such as a festival or fair. These are not only good ideas for building trust in business pursuits but romantic ones as well. Be careful, though, as these may potentially crossover and be hard to distinguish between. Most businesses frown on such behavior, and you risk getting yourself in an unwanted situation where you could not only fail in your seduction but lose your job or face legal ramifications. Once you have successfully built up a level of trust, it's good to do activities that put you and your subject on the same team facing some object to overcome. This is a good tool for team building and relationship building. Be careful though in your choice of activity because as much as you will gain from a shared success, you will lose if the result is a shared failure. Although, in some cases, a shared failure can actually be a stronger solidifier of seduction than a victory, though this is a rare exceptional case.

Step Four: Close the Deal

The fourth and final step is to close the deal. You've already done the work, and your subject is open to your advances. The seduction is almost complete, and all you have to do is reach your goal. This may be establishing a committed relationship, securing a business deal, or being elected to a position. There are steps you can take to increase your chances of success at this stage of the game, but really the key just has the confidence to jump in the deep end and make that final pitch. Your subject has already been primed and may be wondering when you are going to close the deal. The big mistake people make at this point is not to recognize the window of opportunity is open, and the result will be a success as long as you step up to the plate and swing the bat. If you sit on the sidelines too long, not only will you be out of the game, but someone else will take your place on the field. You just need to make your move and strike while the iron is hot. If not, you risk losing out and having the window of opportunity close. If your seduction fails at this point, it is better to get it out of the way and move on with your life and on to the next seduction than to put yourself in a self-made prison while sitting in limbo. The possibility of success is there in front of you, and the risk of failure only makes that success all the sweeter. Even in the event of a failure, it will only add to the joy of victory when you do eventually reach your goals.

Chapter 6: Deception

From the moment we wake up until the moment we lay our heads down to rest drifting off into unconsciousness, we are assaulted by a barrage of lies and deception. The world we live in is filled with double-speak and deceptive language that is meant to manipulate our every action and even our very mental state. The bulk of this deception comes in the form of technology and is done by big tech—but, not to be outdone, the originators and masters of deceptive language are the governments of the world. These governments have been deceiving for thousands of years, and they aren't stopping any time soon. Social media controls what you see in your timeline and steers your mood to up-sell you to their sponsors' advertisements. Mainstream media controls the narrative and deceives the viewers and readers with their lies on a daily, if not hourly, basis giving alerts through apps downloaded onto your personal pocket computer/phone. You must stay up to date on all the latest propaganda and share, like, comment, and subscribe to your technological overlords. Deception layered upon deception sponsored by deception. The media will tell us a lie when we all know the truth, and they will repeat it until you start to question reality.

Adolf Hitler wrote in Mien Kampf, "...in the primitive simplicity of their minds, they more readily fall victims to the big lie than the small lie, as they themselves often tell small lies in little matters but would be ashamed to resort to large-scale falsehoods. It would never come into their heads to fabricate colossal untruths, and they would not believe that others could have the impudence to distort the truth so infamously." In this method of deception, the liar is taking advantage of people's good nature and propensity to be honest. No one is completely honest all the time, but the majority of people do their best to avoid lying and will justify their actions as a means to avoid hurting someone they care for or a way to be non-confrontational if they do tell a lie.

Joseph Goebbels is attributed as having written, "If you tell a lie big enough and keep repeating it, people will eventually come to believe it. The lie can be maintained only for such time as the State can shield the people from the political, economic, and/or military consequences of the lie. It thus becomes vitally important for the State to use all of its powers to repress dissent, for the truth is the mortal enemy of the lie, and thus by extension, the truth is the greatest enemy of the State."

Both Goebbels and Hitler explain the mindset of the liar and how propaganda is used to an effective success, but in both cases, they are not speaking about themselves. They are demonizing their enemies and have deceived themselves into believing that they are righteous and on the side of good versus a deceptive evil. To deceive a nation, they had first to deceive themselves.

This is often the case when dealing with a liar. A liar's first (and sometimes biggest) victim is the person looking them back in the mirror. A liar cannot hold and keep a stable relationship with friends, family, or a significant other. A liar may gain small victories in the short term but will destroy their life in the long term. This forces many liars to be manipulators, and they have little choice but to travel from place to place until they have been discovered as the liar they are and move on to the next community in a never-ending cycle of deceit. This was a more dangerous threat in the past, but in today's age of technology, a liar can be easier to catch. At the same time, many liars use technology as a tool for their manipulations. The difference depends on the individual's ability and skill with modern technology. When looking to detect deception in media and from our government officials, it is essential to be aware of doublespeak. This is a technique originally made famous by George Orwell in his fictional book "1984" and chronicled in real-life usage in the book "Double Speak" by William D. Lutz. Doublespeak can be done to make the harsh truth sound more gentle or to disguise the truth altogether.

When spotting deception on a personal one-on-one level, it is important first to establish a baseline with your subject. Many of the tell-tale signs of deception appear to the novice as a red flag, and they very well may probably be, but to the trained expert, these are false flags. What this means is that any individual deception marker expressed in and of itself does not constitute a positive reading on our human lie detector test. One raindrop does not make a puddle, and one deception identifier does not equal a lie. In order to accurately spot a deception, it is necessary to detect multiple red flags to indicate a lie. When you see someone touching their face while looking down and away, avoiding the question, then getting aggressive and angry, all the while pointing their feet at the nearest exit, you have got yourself a surefire liar. But if you only spot one of these behaviors, it is not necessarily a sign of deception but more likely a sign of nervousness and likely innocence. Why would a person be nervous if they are not deceptive? In many situations, a person can be nervous for any number of reasons, some of which may have nothing to do with the situation whatsoever.

Another key to spotting deception is to attempt to wrest control of the conversation away from the other person. If this not possible, there is a good chance you are dealing with a liar. Liars will often monopolize the conversation to control the narrative and not let you get a word in edgewise. But not all liars embody this trait, and the more skilled liar will let you control the conversation. This lightens their burden of keeping up such a high energy level as is demanded when over-talking others into submission. When in control of the conversation after establishing the baseline of your subject and lulling them into a false sense of security and confidence, you can use the element of surprise to your advantage. In the initial moments after asking someone a question, their mind does not have the time to think fast enough to develop a deception or the ability to mask all physical tells. It is in these moments that you will get your best chance to spot the deception. A trained liar or someone who watches a few videos or reads a few blogs may be arrogant enough to think they can just stall by freezing at the moment after a question is asked of them, but an experienced investigator looks for this behavior as a red flag. Stalling, in general, is a sign of deception when someone repeats a question back to you or asks you to repeat a question they are likely buying time to develop a deception, but they could just be hard of hearing. Aggressive behavior is one of the best indicators in spotting deception. When someone is showing signs of anger that you would even ask them a question, it is a tip-off that they are being defensive and are trying to hide something. This is an attempt to control you using fear and scare you away from further inquiry. If your subject gets angry, it is best not to continue, but to defuse the situation and calm them down.

Once you have spotted a deception, it is not a given that you will not fall prey to its charm. Deception is not always blunt and harsh but often a delight until the reality sets in. Many deceptions comfort us and make us feel safe; these deceptions take advantage of us on many levels and prey upon our need to feel this way. When faced with deception online, doing something as simple and minimal as a 'thumbs down' can defend against future deceptions. By thumbing down a video or post, you are less likely to be confronted with this same deception, at least from that same source. The thumbs-down also serves the purpose of indicating to others that this post is a deception. When you see a video or post that has a low like-to-dislike ratio, you know something is rotten in Denmark—or is it Sweden? You can also leave a comment if you wish, but this is considered positive engagement regardless of how negative the comment, even if you point out the author of the post or creator of the video to be a complete fraud and scam artist deceiving people out of their hard earn money. Leaving comments on videos all day is a futile effort. That is not to say, don't share your opinion, but caution to not get carried away trying to save the world one mean comment at a time.

When it comes to your personal and professional life, you can have a much more profound effect in defending against deception. Use extreme caution, though, when attempting to spot deception from a loved one. The last thing you want to do in a relationship is to (falsely) accuse someone you are close to lying to you. You need to be absolutely sure because there is a great chance that you will be not only risking your relationship but bringing it to an end. It may not end right then and there, but if you falsely accuse a loved one of lying, it is an injury not quickly forgot nor forgiven. You may be speaking to that person for the last time. The same goes for business—if you accuse a business partner of deception, they will likely either quit or want you fired. A potential sale accused of deception will hang up or walk out the door. So use discretion and be subtle when necessary, and if there is any doubt, it is best to give loved ones the benefit of the doubt. But in defense of yourself, do not let your love blind you from obvious truths right in front of your eyes. A deceiver will take advantage of your emotional connection, whether it is on a friendly level or one more intimate. When having any doubts, it helps to talk out the situation with a neutral party who is outside of it and can help you see it from a big-picture perspective. Oftentimes, it's easy to get too close to a deceiver to defend against their deception even after making a positive detection. Sometimes, it is best to create space between you and the deceiver so they cannot manipulate your emotions and desires for them to be truthful. In this type of situation, it is best to confront them about the deception with trusted friends or family members at your side. There is strength in numbers when defending against a deceiver. But you may not be in a position to call upon anyone else and need to rely only on yourself. If this is the case, then your best defense against being deceived is to acknowledge the truth and hold it dear. In other words, believe in the truth for he who stands for nothing falls for anything. If you are doubtful, you are open to deception. But if you know the truth and believe in the truth, then you can fight off deception in all its forms.

Chapter 7: The Art of Reading People

Reading and understanding non-verbal communication is an essential life skill that some people seem to do innately, while others need to put great effort into it for even limited ability to execute. Most people in the "First World" fall somewhere between these extremes. A good comprehension of non-verbal communication is an asset and arguably integral to our inter-personal relations.

Non-verbal communication (NVC) is any information exchanged that is not transmitted by language and includes what is heard, seen, and felt through touch.

Being aware of non-verbal cues not only helps you to read others but also to help us provide non-verbal cues for others to read.

In auditory NVC, listening not only to the words but to the tonality, inflections, and volume can give you valuable information. It is also important to mentally acknowledge the level/form of language used and mirror it if possible. This serves not only to maintain the status quo but may be necessary for the listener to understand. Characteristics of the spoken word beyond its linguistic meaning are known as paralanguage.

- Tonality – an important part of interpersonal communication. Consider the following statement: 'I'll get right on that boss.' The tone with which this sentence is communicated will determine if the statement is sincere, begrudging, eager, or sarcastic. If you were the speaker in the scenario, the tone could have serious consequences. As a listener, the tone gives valuable information about the emotion or sentiment behind the words.

- Inflection – the emphasis is in words, what word or words were accentuated, or de-emphasized. This helps the listener determine the importance of something to or the feeling the speaker is trying to convey.

- Volume – this can help to indicate the emotional state of the speaker. Loud, boisterous language can be due to excitement, anger, happiness, or frustration. As the listener, it is important to determine which of these the speaker is trying to express.

- Speed – The speed of speech is affected by not only emotional state and the sentimentality of the words but also by a wide variety of other things—a person's age, mental health, cognitive ability, comfortability with the language spoken, and the use of various drugs (prescription and illicit). A person may be speaking fast while under the influence of cocaine, amphetamines, or other "uppers" or they may be a mentally ill patient in the midst of a manic phase. Conmen and unethical salespersons will intentionally talk faster than most people can understand in an effort to manipulate the mark.

Physical touch and physical proximity are methods of non-verbal communication. A person could use close physical proximity and perhaps even touch to indicate interest, a desire not to be overheard by others, friendliness, compassion, etc. Alternately, close physical proximity can be a sign of aggression, anger, or some malevolent interest (to rob, harass, or assault). A large distance between speaker and listener can simply be mechanical (physical impediment like reception desk) in nature. It can also indicate negative feelings towards or between the 2 communicators such as fear, resentment, anger, or even disgust. A lack of familiarity could also be a factor in how close someone is comfortable with the other person. Changes in physical proximity are important indicators of the "barometer" of the conversation. Is the distance between the 2 participants increasing or decreasing? An increase in distance between listener and speaker is usually not a favorable sign. One participant may be trying to end a conversation for any of a variety of reasons and does not want to be rude. One participant may have become fearful, distrustful, disgusted, or frustrated and wants to increase the distance between the participants. We learn as children the difference between good and bad touch. In non-verbal communication, physical touch, and the subsequent reaction to the touch can give each person a strong indication of the sentiment or barometer of the interaction. In professional relationships and in situations between individuals who are not so familiar yet, caution should be used when physically touching another, and careful attention is necessary to gauge the reaction of the recipient of the touch, particularly if the reaction is negative.

The bulk of the information we receive through non-verbal means is visual.

There are both conscious, as well as unconscious, non-verbal cues; it is very difficult for a person to learn to control the cues we are conscious of and nearly impossible for the unconscious (notable exception medical interventions available to "cure" uncontrolled idiopathic blushing). A common colloquialism about reading the room is good advice for someone interested in non-verbal communication. In this case, I am referring to taking in things like the environment and setting as well as observing the participants. It is especially important in situations that may elicit strong emotional responses. If you need to break the bad news to someone doing so in a loud, crowded area is not ideal. Inviting the person to a quiet location away from the masses is preferred (assuming the listener is amenable to this). If you have news, you have to tell the listener that you feel will make them angry you should not impart the information in a busy area, but be mindful of your safety. Being within sight or hearing of others is often prudent. Again, physical proximity is an important determinant in reading an interaction.

Posture is a good indicator of the feelings of the individuals going into and throughout the interaction. Arms crossed tend to be seen as a negative reaction or project a negative emotion (unless, of course, it is because the individual is cold). In reality, experts in reading body language identify the crossing of one's arms as a mechanism of self-soothing, or in layman's terms a self-hug. This is done to provide the self-soother with a sense of security in a tense situation, not unlike a child clinging to their blanket.

Open, relaxed arms are commonly seen as having a correlation to positive feelings towards communication. When it may just be a sign of the speaker's confidence—open tense arms could indicate some sort of distress, fear, or anger, for example. Most communication seminars and classes recommend mirroring or reflecting the posture of the other participant in your interaction. Posture can include sitting versus standing – trying to be at the same level is ideal for communication. This suggests feelings of equality (no one higher than the other) and the desire for positive interaction. It also allows for eye contact, an important non-verbal communication tool, which will be discussed later in this chapter.

Gestures are important sources of information in interpersonal communication. Notably, the hand gesture generally accepted as OK to most English-speaking North Americans; it is the equivalent of "flipping the bird" in Brazil. In many Middle Eastern and Mediterranean countries, it is one of several insults that originated because of the gestures' resemblance to the anus and is considered a threat in some Arab countries.

We all have likely known and interacted with a person that is not judicious with their use of arm gestures, and the more excited or worked up the individual became, the arm gestures increased. In general arm gestures are not the best predictor of how the interaction is going because of the expansive individual differences in the degree of intensity does not necessarily translate correctly.

Facial expressions are the key to reading most people. Persons able to master the so-called poker face are one big exception. The term poker face is used to describe a face completely devoid of emotion and unreactive to outside stimuli; it originates from people that are able to hide their true feelings when dealt a hand. A good poker face is crucial for a gambler to bluff their hand successfully. In this case, it is easier to disguise a good poker hand than it is to project a good hand when holding losing cards. When dealt a royal straight flush, the instinctual reaction of the majority of people is akin to that of having just won the lottery or first prize in a competition. The veteran poker player will suppress this reaction and keep a straight face so as not to tip off their opponent that they should fold the hand, instead drawing them in to bet and raise their bet by giving them a false sense of security by withholding the information a less experienced player will have communicated through non-verbal cues. When bluffing a bad hand, the player must convince their opponent that they have a better hand than the one they are holding. It is much more difficult to manufacture false nonverbal cues to deceive the opponent into folding and is more often done in subtler ways by using the number of chips bet to convey a false sense of confidence with one's hand. The player in the case of the bluff is easily stopped by a veteran when attempting to convey a false sense of confidence in their hand with false nonverbal cues and body language. Oftentimes, the bluffer overdoes the expression of false emotion to a comical level that the veteran player instantly picks up on and calls All In. The veteran poker player is more likely to stay at a baseline of expression and not converge away from this level of emotion. They will let their chips do the talking for them as they bluff with their betting practices from hand to hand. There are exceptions, and on occasion, the poker world will see a flashy rising star come in with a brash personality, almost bullying their way to victory using aggressive body language and nonverbal communication. This usually leads to a short career with a varying amount of success within that time frame, eventually leading to burnout as the player's luck runs out. The flaw in this approach is that while it may work in the short term, long term the experienced veterans will study the brash player's baseline and develop the ability to spot the unconventional cues given off by this type of player. This player's cues, while difficult to spot the first time around because of the lack of information when reading their baseline, will be the easiest player to read the next time a veteran player comes up against them at the table. The ability to establish a decent poker face is quite difficult for most people. The human is reported to be able to generate over ten thousand different expressions.

Reading facial expressions can be challenging, especially with people you are not familiar with. Eye Contact is also a good gauge for non-verbal communication. Eye contact is a must in situations such as job interviews. Persons that avoid eye contact are often thought of as suspicious or shifty and to be hiding something. Intense eye contact can occur in interactions with intense emotions such as love or hate, anger, or lust. A person can use penetrating eye contact to instill fear and coerce the recipient into submission. A piercing gaze can indicate sexual attraction and desire. Making direct, but not intense, eye contact when communicating is considered polite in North American culture. In some other cultures, it is considered rude or as a challenge. In the Animal Kingdom, many species respond to direct eye contact as a threat or challenge. Eye contact allows us to read more information beyond the act itself. The eyes are famously known as windows to our soul and will betray us if we lie. The autonomic nervous system, which is in control of the sympathetic nervous system (and the parasympathetic nervous system), will trigger the "flight or fight" response in the sympathetic nervous system if a strong emotion of attraction (physical)/arousal, fear, or anger. One of the consequences of the fight or flight response is the dilation (opening) of our pupils. Eye contact allows us to monitor for pupil dilation, thereby predicting how the other participant is feeling. It is important to note here that there are other natural and pathological reasons for pupil dilation; and even if the pupillary dilation is because of the activation of the sympathetic nervous system, it only tells us that one or more of the possible emotions have been evoked. Mistakenly thinking that the dilated pupils signified sexual arousal or physical attraction could have unpleasant ramifications. Certain medical conditions and drugs can cause eyes to be dilated, which can cause confusion when reading the non-verbal cue. The autonomic nervous system, in response to dimming light, also will cause eyes to dilate. This response is independent of the 'fight or flight' response. The dilation or widening of the pupils is designed to allow more light to reach the retina when it gets darker to help us see. Many vertebrate (have a spine) animals have an extra layer in the eye called the tapetum. The tapetum is reflective and increases the ability of the animal to see in the dark. If you have ever noticed how a pet's eyes seem to glow in the dark or seen the spooky shiny spots at the side of a rural road when driving at night, you have seen the reflective tapetum of an animal at work. Interestingly, this layer that was designed to aid and protect the animal can quickly hasten its doom. An animal with a tapetum that is exposed to bright light suddenly becomes blind, dazed, and disoriented. We have all experienced the blindness associated with abrupt assault of turning on a light in the darkness; the degree of blindness is much greater in creatures with a tapetum.

There is a controversial hunting method that exploits the tapetum, often referred to as spotlighting or lamping. Many states and provinces have laws either limiting or prohibiting the practice. Hunters go out at night to hunt nocturnal game (badgers, hares, rabbits, foxes, and deer during hunting season) usually on some variety of off-road vehicle, and usually in a group. Bright flashlights or spotlights are directed at the prey to blind and disorient them, also to highlight their location. Deer become nocturnal when the hunting season is active in a means to protect themselves. Hunting deer with spotlights is illegal in many places.

There are cultural differences in non-verbal communication. Some tribes put more of an emphasis on hand gestures than other cultures. As discussed above, hand gestures may have vastly different meanings in different cultures. It is wise to research before using hand gestures while traveling in a foreign country.

Gangs use hand gestures to communicate gang affiliation and to antagonize rival gang members into confrontations; caution should be used when using hand gestures in an unfamiliar environment. In the case of gang members throwing hand signs can be non-confrontational in certain settings and used to express joy or celebration by the gang member. In most situations, though, this is far from the intention of the expression. More commonly, gang signs are used to declare which gang one belongs to and what set they claim. When a gang member comes across a person whom they are unfamiliar with inside of their territory customarily, they will toss up their gang sign and throw down a rival's sign to see if this action elicits a response from the stranger. The gang member is now reading nonverbal cues to determine if the stranger to the hood is a threat or a mark. Depending on this reading, the gang member may take a variety of actions. If the stranger is seen to be a threat, violence will ensue. If this threat is read as a rival gang member, then the violence too often reaches deathly proportions. If the stranger is seen to be a mark, the gang member will either rob them on the spot or engage with them to gather more information to determine the opportune time to make the most out of this potentially profitable situation. The gang member may turn this stranger into a customer for any number of illegal substances depending upon this reading of body language and non-verbal cues. The stranger may show signs of drug withdrawal leading the gang member to feel secure in selling them drugs at the risk that this stranger is potentially an undercover cop. A mistake in reading non-verbal cues and body language in this situation can lead to a lifetime behind bars for the gang member. This makes reading body language and non-verbal cues and essential tool for survival among gang members and street criminals. Those that have become incarcerated must have an even higher level of understanding and expressing such cues as they are at even great risk. In an incarceration situation, the inmate is in close quarters twenty-four hours a day, seven days a week, three hundred and sixty-five days a year. Inside of these close quarters with them are all manner of criminals, both low-level offenders and extremely dangerous violent psychopaths. To survive this environment, the

118

ability to read body language and non-verbal cues is a necessity. Those that do not develop this talent will suffer severe penalties, most likely leading to their death. Conversely, even a nonviolent offender can survive this harsh environment by learning these tools for reading body language and non-verbal communication. In such dangerous situations and environments, it is always advised to an error on the side of caution for safety's sake. When assessing a threat, if it appears to be a high level, whether or not it truly is, it is best to act accordingly and take precautions. An example of this would be if you read the body language of a would attacker to be aggressive it may not mean they are about to strike out in a violent rage, but it would be ill-advised to goad them into action by triggering them with your own body language and non-verbal cues. Instead, send out cues that put this potential attacker at ease as you slowly and calmly make your way to an exit or attract the attention of others around to avert the attention of the aggressor away from you.

There has been a method of child-rearing that involves teaching children hand gestures to facilitate communicating with them before they are talking. It allows the child to communicate their desires before they can verbalize them.

Entertainers, as well as politicians, are advised to play to their audience. In non-verbal communication, it is important to be aware of who your audience is and adjust accordingly in the same way as in verbal communication.

When it comes to reading Body language cues and understanding how to interpret them, it is important first to surmise whether the person communicating is well versed in Dark Psychology or a layman. When reading a layman, the cues are easier to interpret due to the subject's lack of knowledge in the cues they are sending. Someone more informed on the techniques described within this book will be harder to read because of a conscious effort to disguise the cues that communicate their secret motivation. It is not impossible to read such a person's body language cues, but determining the level of education regarding Dark Psychology is extremely difficult unless coerced in some way or freely admitted. Even in the case of the layman, it is possible to misread body language cues due to a lack of information on the subject being read. A physical condition, either permanent or temporary, can affect the subject's physical body language. Pain caused by stomach ache or abdominal cramp can be misinterpreted as disgust—when, in actuality, the subject had mild food poisoning or Crohn's disease.

Reading body language can also be lifesaving when facing a dangerous situation whether or not the threat is real or imagined. If you pick up on non-verbal cues that lead you to believe a person on the street is about to mug you, whether or not this is an accurate reading of the cues, the action that is taken next could prevent you from being a victim of a crime. A person in a public park can be misread by a criminal as having something valuable to steal, and the criminal approaches the would-be victim to gather more information on the potential prey. The predator asks the potential prey if they want to buy drugs as a way of seeing if the target has money. The subject of the questioning responds that they have no money, whether true or false, the criminal may interpret the non-verbal cues through confirmation bias due to a need for the victim to have something of value to steal. The potential victim of the crime may be unaware that although they may or may not be telling the truth to the criminal, the predator has already misread their body language and has determined that they will prey on the victim; and that it will be worth their effort. It is only after attacking the victim of the crime and finding out that they misread their subject that the criminal is faced with the reality of the situation. This will anger the predator and can lead to a life-threatening situation and an escalation of the violence perpetrated upon the victim. In this situation, if the victim realizes that the criminal is preparing to attack regardless of their response to questioning, the victim may have a small window of opportunity to exit the situation and create space between themselves and their predator before the crime can occur. In this situation, it is best to not only create distance from a would-be attacker but to get to an area where there may be armed security or police surveillance to deter the predator. The more people around, the less likely a predator will strike in most cases. The worst place to run is a dark, secluded area, such as an alley. Running in and of itself should be done with caution as well, for it may encourage the predator to chase; walking at a brisk pace is a safer way to create space between the victim and the would-be attacker. In some cases, a would-be attacker will close the gap between themselves and their potential victim and use intimidating body language while verbally asking their victim to attack them physically first. This is done out of a false sense of morality by the predator who does not want to see themselves as the bad guy and needs their victim to wrong them in some perceived manner before their conscious can justify their criminal actions, though this is a rare case. Still, it is common for predators to justify their actions with "they were asking for it" in reference to their victims.

Sexual predators often justify their actions to the authority upon interrogation with claims of being sent nonverbal cues by their victims. These predators often have trouble reading social cues, to begin with, and through their psychoses continue to misread body language knowingly or unknowingly to rationalize their behavior. These offenders not only manipulate their victims but themselves through mental gymnastics. This may occur on a subconscious or unconscious level. New studies show that the hard wiring of the brain in certain violent criminals makes it impossible for them to interpret social cues and body language correctly. This does not mean that a lack of skill in reading nonverbal communication leads one to violent crime as the average person has relatively little expertise in reading such cues.

On the other side of the law, police are put in life and death situations on a daily basis where reading a person's body language can be the difference between going home to their loved one or ones at the end of the shift, and making an unexpected trip to the morgue, in a body bag. Every time a law enforcement officer approaches a person while on the job, the risk exists that the confrontation could end lethally on either end. A typical traffic stop too often results in either an officer being shot or an officer shooting a suspect. Being able to read nonverbal cues can buy the officer enough time, even a split second can make the difference in the outcome, to react in defense of their life. As an officer of the law approaches a vehicle on a routine stop, they must evaluate if the suspect is following order to place their hands on their steering wheel, among other requests. Compliance with instructions shows the suspect's willingness to cooperate and lowers the threat assessment. But until the traffic stop is complete, the officer cannot let their guard down until all parties involved are secured safely. An officer initially may be given compliance only to find that the suspect is buying time, waiting for a moment of perceived advantage over the officer in the situation before making a move. This can be in the form of a violent attack or taking off on the run, whether in a vehicle or by making a run for it literally on foot. Not only does the officer have to make quick evaluations of the perceived body language of the driver but the passengers as well. As soon as a driver pulls over, it is not uncommon for a passenger of the vehicle to take off on foot. Sometimes, this may be due to the passenger having warrants or being a known suspect in a prior crime. The passenger may be in possession of illegal goods such as narcotics or stolen property. In either case, a fleeing suspect may potentially be armed and dangerous. In this heightened situation, the stress levels of all involved are raised to high levels, and any sudden movement can be interpreted by either party involved as a violent threat of action. A fleeing suspect may only be in possession of a joint of Marijuana or stolen shoes and reaching for their phone to call for a getaway ride. This same suspect could just as easily be high on crystal meth and in possession of a high caliber firearm. Signs such as shaky hands or excessive sweating can be tip-offs to the suspect's mental state and are taken into account when making a threat assessment. But it is natural for a person to be nervous when confronted by an officer of the law, the shaky hands and excessive sweating may just be nerves from fear of the police due to reading too many stories in the news about the police shooting innocent victims, whether or not these stories have credibility or not. Either way, the officer cannot risk ignoring warning signs and will likely place the suspect in handcuffs and possibly in the back of their cruiser until the situation has been fully assessed and secured. Once the suspect has been cleared for risk of threat and any tickets have been issued, if necessary, the officer can safely remove the handcuffs and return the suspect to their vehicle. This may seem excessive if no threat is found, and it is merely a routine traffic stop with a minor infraction warranting only a ticket. On the other hand, if a weapon is found in the vehicle or evidence of another crime, then the measure taken seem less extreme. If the officer had not taken what may seem like extreme measures in one circumstance, the situation could escalate into an opportunity for the suspect to make a grave mistake that could result to the end of their life, the life of the officer, or all parties involved in the traffic stop.

Law enforcement officers use their skills at reading nonverbal communication in all of their interactions with criminals to varying degrees of success. In some cases, these skills are used in conjunction with Dark Psychology Techniques as described earlier in the book. During an interrogation of a suspect, a detective will use their skill at reading body language when practicing techniques such as fatigue inducement. The non-verbal cues can signify to the interrogator when the suspect is about to break down, and give either valuable information, or a confession with just the right technique applied at the opportune moment. Before the interrogator can read the suspect's body language and non-verbal cues, they must first establish the baseline of the suspect. This is done by first easing the suspect into a false sense of security. The interrogator asks simple, non-threatening questions to control the suspect's stress levels. The interrogator will often agree with the suspect and ensure them that they have done nothing wrong, and this is just an information-gathering exercise to help the interrogator clear them of any and all wrongdoing. The interrogator may ask questions of the suspect that seem very out of place for the situation, such as what is the suspect's favorite sports team, movie, or music artist. The interrogator may try to establish a bond over the responses to these questions by agreeing that they also love the same movie or sports team. Conversely, the interrogator may give a negative response to the suspect's answer and exclaim that their favorite music artist is garbage just to see the reaction given by the suspect when confronted with the disagreement of something they hold value in. Once a baseline has been established, the interrogator can determine whether certain non-verbal cues are normal behavior for the suspect or abnormal and a red flag. Increased touching of one's face shows a nervousness on the part of the suspect. The higher on the face a person touches themselves, the more nervous energy within they are trying to control. Touching the face is also another example of self-soothing. Constant movements can at first be an exertion of pent up energy, but as the interrogation continues, it can be a sign of fatigue and an attempt by the suspect to keep themselves sharp to avoid a slip-up, or from falling asleep. Lack of eye contact reveals an attempt to hide information from the interrogator or shame for the crime committed. Sometimes, this shame can result not from having committed the crime but from not having prevented the crime and is a result of feeling guilty. When a suspect's eyes dart around the room, they are looking for inspiration to create a lie or looking for a way out of the situation. When a person looks to the right, they are accessing auditory memory of what they heard. When looking to the left, the suspect is accessing visual memory of what they saw. When looking down and to the right, they are accessing the creative part of their brain in an attempt to make up a believable story potentially or to use the creative part of their brain to fill in gaps of memory. When looking down and to the left, the suspect is attempting to isolate themselves from reality, possibly in an attempt to relive the memory or an attempt to shut it out. Without establishing a proper baseline, these cues can be falsely interpreted and miscommunicated. Just as in the case of a lie detector, these methods are not infallible, nor are they admissible in court. This is why it takes a skilled professional, and even then, a confession of guilt is needed without further physical evidence to convict a suspect of a crime.

Chapter 8: Master Your Emotions

How to Transform and Manage Your Emotions

Mastering your emotions can be a difficult process and seemly impossible to some. Before describing techniques to master your emotions, we will explore the 10 types of emotional manipulators. This will allow us to gain insight into how these manipulators use both our emotions and theirs to control the desired result. By learning how these manipulators work, we can identify them and defend against them. Here is a list of the most commonly recognized emotional manipulators, in no particular order:

- The Projector

- The Iron Fist

- Triangulators

- The Deliberate Misinterpreter

- The Flirt

- The Constant Victim

- Powerful Dependents

- The One-Upmanship Expert

- The Blaster

- The Multiple Offender

The Projector

This type of emotional manipulator projects their feelings onto others. The Projector will also assign blame to those around them when faced with failures. Nothing is ever the fault of the Projector, it is always your fault in their eyes, and they will use gaslighting tactics to confuse and distort reality. By the end of an interaction with a projector, you may find yourself questioning what really happened and if you are the one to blame even though you know beyond a doubt that they are the ones to blame. The Projector is also a master of self-manipulation and creates their own reality before forcing it on their targets of manipulation. These manipulators are masters of creating doubt in the minds of their victims.

The Iron Fist

This type of emotional manipulator uses subtle and not so subtle forms of aggression to manipulate their victims through fear. The Iron Fist will make you an offer you cannot refuse. Oftentimes, the Iron Fist defines the terms among their victims and sets clear guidelines for what they deem to be acceptable behavior. If you step outside this approved behavior, the Iron Fist will deliver the promised punishment to not only reinforce their power and control over the victim but to use the situation as a means of deterring similar behavior from others in and outside the relationship. Iron Fist commonly seeks out a position of authority to live out their power fantasies and to control victims.

Triangulators

This type of manipulator uses gossip to control groups of people. They will isolate their victims to a one-on-one situation and then degrade and belittle someone or a group of people not present in

130

the interaction. Triangulators will feed into a person's ego during this process by building them up as they tear down the object of their slander. This is done often as a way to deflect blame away from the Triangulator and on to another party. Then, when interacting with the slandered target, the Triangulator will shift the blame on the previous person in the situation and heap praise on the current victim. Triangulators will often use kernels of truth in an attempt to create tension and conflict among a group. Another way of describing Triangulators is as instigators. It is likely that you have experienced this situation and seen a Triangulator instigate a conflict to create drama while avoiding any confrontation by the offended parties involved. These are people who start drama and walk away before the shit hits the fan.

The Deliberate Misinterpreter

This type of manipulator will use your words against you by twisting their meaning to fit their agenda. We often see this type of manipulator incorporate another method. The Deliberate Misinterpreter will take any, and all information externally received and bent it to their preconceived world view. We all have our biases, but this type of manipulator is closed to any information that contradicts their mindset and is incredibly stubborn. The Deliberate Misinterpreter will take information that clearly debunks their interpretation and use it as evidence for their argument. In personal social interactions, they will use their victim's words to hang themselves and gaslight their victims into apologizing while creating self-doubt in the targets of their manipulation. If you find yourself apologizing for something you did or said that did not warrant an apology you like are Canadian or dealing with a Deliberate Misinterpreter.

The Flirt

This type of manipulator uses the technique of seduction to manipulate their victim, as earlier discussed in Chapter 5 of this book. The Flirt will use their attractiveness to make you feel attractive. They are masters of seduction and will tease their victims with promises of future positive reactions upon receipt of rewards in the present. The Flirt makes its victims feel special at the moment while interacting with them until their goals are accomplished within the situation. Once the Flirt has what they want, they will shut down and end the interaction in any number of ways, all the while leaving the door open for future manipulation, often with a promise serving as an emotional cliffhanger for their victims. It is only once the Flirt is away from their victim that the victim realizes they have been manipulated into sacrificing themselves for the Flirts gain. The victim of the Flirt is not always aware of the manipulation due to the strong use of emotional control by the Flirt to cloud the judgment of their victims, or in other words, "blind them with love." Even when the victim becomes aware of the spell they are under, it is difficult for the victim to keep a clear mindset in the presence of the Flirt. The Flirt, as a type of emotional manipulator, is not a blanket description of all people who flirt but rather those that overuse an innocent social interaction to accomplish their goals through manipulation. It is the common use of flirting as a social tool for interaction that the Flirt uses to exploit their victims and catch them off guard to establish an abusive relationship of all give and no take. Sometimes, the Flirt will imitate a giving to manipulate their victim into believing that the relationship is not a one-way street. But in reality, the Flirt is only giving what they have either previously taken or that which has little to no value in their world.

The Constant Victim

This type of manipulator has become increasingly common in today's society, as seemingly daily, there is a public example of the Constant Victim on display. This is one of the easier types to identify due to the regularity in which we are confronted with this type of manipulation. Traditionally this type of manipulator was found among the younger members of society and has been described as acting "like a baby" or "a child." The Constant Victim casts themselves in the role of victim in every situation, even those of their own making. They whine and complain and assign blame in their game of manipulation. The Constant Victim will go so far as to attribute blame to God for the very rain on a cold November day and play victim to the natural changing of seasons in their environment as if the entirety of existence is out to get them. The Constant Victim often has symptoms of paranoia and can develop into a full-blown paranoid schizophrenic left untreated. The Constant Victim will use their victim status to garner sympathy from their victims.

This is another gaslighting technique, which is a common fixture among the types of manipulators. They use gaslighting to bend reality and the perception of truth in the minds of their victims to gain leverage in the situation. In today's society, victim status is worshipped and praised as being beyond reproach and investigation. This encourages this type of manipulator's behavior in a desire to gain fame, fortune, and social status. The

Constant Victim was traditionally looked at as the "boy who cried wolf" but with the shift in societies perception and values the Constant Victim has gone from one of the more harmless types of manipulators to being one of the more dangerous in the sheer scope and magnitude of their influence and manipulation that is prevalent in this day and age.

Powerful Dependents

This type of manipulator sounds like an oxymoron, a contradiction in terms, but they are instead a skilled master of deception. Powerful dependents mask their strength and portray a weak face to their victim and in public. There is some crossover between the Powerful Dependents and the Constant Victim, but the crossover is not uncommon among the types of manipulators as we shall explore with Multiple Offenders. Powerful Dependents develop parasitic relationships with their victims and take on the role of a dependent on passing their responsibilities. Powerful Dependents are generally and more commonly thought of and found in personal relationships. These manipulators use close relationships to assign guilt to those who care about them in an effort to manipulate them for all of their needs. Some Powerful Dependents develop whole networks of victims to support their wants and needs in life. This can happen on a much larger scale, as in the case of the 2008 bailout of the big banks explored earlier in the book. Wall Street and the Big Banks came to the United States Government and took on the role of a dependent and guilted the representatives of the people into bailing them out with 700 billion dollars of the taxpayers' money. Politicians, Preachers, Podcasters, Television, and Internet hosts alike will play the role of dependent on their audience to manipulate financial support from their victims.

The One-Upmanship Expert

This type of manipulator will always attempt to outshine those around them. The One-Upmanship Expert is a common manipulator that you have likely come across. You likely know someone who, when made aware of your success or the success of another, has to tell you of a time when they did something similar but better than you. If you announce in the presence of the One-Upmanship that you got an A, top-grade, on your test or evaluation, this manipulator will proclaim to have gotten an A+ on the test or on a prior test that was much more difficult than what they describe as "easy" test you scored a high grade on. If a One-Upmanship Expert hears that a top athlete in professional sports has had a huge game, they will tell a story of a time in the past when they put up far superior numbers. They may not have even participated in physical athletics of any kind and even view virtual accomplishments as being superior to real-world triumphs. The One-Upmanship Expert needs the spotlight to be on them at all times and sees themselves as the center of the universe. They will not allow their victims to have positive attention in their presence and tear down those around them in an attempt to build themselves up.

The Blaster

This type of manipulator is often confused with the Iron Fist as they both use aggressive behavior. The difference being that the Blaster will use their aggression as a tool to dominate a situation by using Fatigue Inducement, as discussed in Chapter 2. The Blaster will take over a situation and conversation. They will not let you get in a word edgewise. This is another gaslighting technique use to manipulate you through sheer exhaustion. By the end of a conversation with a Blaster, you may not know what's up and down and are questioning your prior perception of the reality of the situation. Blasters control you through verbal force but commonly use physical techniques to force their point or keep your attention focused on them. A Blaster may use the clapping of hands and even punch their hands to create noise and a show of strength to control their victim. But Blasters are not always so overhanded and forceful with their aggressive behavior. Some Blasters will use a subtler approach and kill you with a seeming kindness as they lull you into submission. They dominate conversations and interactions with their stamina but with a gentler touch and softer voice to avoid being detected. These are Master Blaster's and, once recognized, should be avoided at all costs. Luckily they are rare, and you are more likely to come across a garden variety Blaster that will be easy to spot.

The Multiple Offender

If you are confused as to which type of manipulator you are dealing with, it is likely that they are a Multiple Offender. This type of manipulator will implore multiple types of manipulation techniques and switch in a very fluid manner between them. As you have recognized, there is a crossover between the types of manipulators, and many do exhibit similar, if not the same, tactics. This can get confusing, but that is a red flag alerting you that you are dealing with a master of manipulation in the form of a Multiple Offender. This type of manipulator is very dangerous to your mental (and possibly physical) health. What makes them so dangerous is their expertise and lack of remorse. The Multiple Offender is, at best, a borderline psychopath and can embody some if not all of the negative traits described throughout this book. These manipulators often have high intelligence and think of themselves as being superior to their victims.

Managing Our Emotions

Now that we have identified the types of emotional manipulators, we will explore how to manage our emotions and transform our emotional state. By mastering our emotions, we can defend against the use of the Dark Psychological Technique to manipulate our minds. Emotions are integral, unavoidable reactions in human existence. Emotions are sensations or feelings that are a product of our environment, interactions with others, or even our own thoughts. Emotions are controlled within our body by our nervous system through hormone regulation. The release or suppression of these chemicals causes both physical and mental changes that translate to our emotional state or reaction. Although we may not be able to avoid having emotions, we can learn to control our reactions to these emotions, both internally and externally. And we will learn how to transform our emotional state towards the desired result.

Charles Darwin was the first to use photographs in a Scientific Publication to record the presence of facial expressions in both humans and animals. Facial expression is a good predictor of mood in most people. Being aware and mindful of this, we can aim to control our facial expressions to mask our emotions from those around us. As discussed earlier, people with extreme control of their facial expressions are often labeled as having a good "poker face."

But to really master our emotions, we must not merely mask them but transform them altogether. This starts through recognition of how we create emotions on a subconscious level and what stimuli do trigger an emotional state. Our environment is one such trigger; this stimulus is an external source of emotion which one may or may not have any control over. If you have control of your environment, you can change it to create a better emotional state. In Chinese culture, this is a practice known as Feng Shui, a system of laws considered to govern spatial arrangement and orientation in relation to the flow of energy. By taking control of your environment, you are creating your own reality in a positive light to stimulate a desired emotional reaction to one of the 3 major stimuli.

Not everyone has control of their environment, but this does not mean that all hope is lost. If in a situation where you cannot control your environment, you can change your perception of the environment. This is not recommended as it is a form of self-deception and can lead to negative effects and consequences. In reality, choices are not always between right and wrong; sometimes, the choice is between wrong and worse. This is more common in the choice between political candidates running for public office. If you feel you cannot control your environment and must resort to self-deception, stop, and seek out help and explore all of your options first. Do not just lazily resort to a dangerous technique that, when done out of sloth, will most definitely not bring about your desired goal. When changing your perception of reality to control the emotional stimuli from your environment, you must highlight only the positive of the situation. This is similar to looking on the bright side of life or finding the silver lining in a grey rain cloud. Sounds harmless enough, but at its core, it is self-deception. It is good to see the positive around you but not at the expensive of reality. In this case, reality takes a back seat to the desire for emotional control over your environment. If you have taken it this far, get yourself into a better environment and cease with the use of this technique before you do further damage to your mental health and seek out help from a professional.

Another stimulus that affects our emotional state is our interactions with others. Not unlike the previous stimuli, the environment, we seldom have control over our interactions with others. What we do control is our perception of these interactions. In some interactions, we can control whether or not they take place at all. If any of these interactions produce undesired emotions, it is best when possible to cease having interactions with the person who creates a negative stimulus in our emotional state. But in situations where we cannot control, not only if an interaction takes place, but the regularity upon which we may have to interact with a person who stimulates negative emotions within us, it is important to control our perceptions of the stimuli. In these interactions, we will bring our own preconceived bias with us. This bias informs whether or not we read the interaction as positive or negative. Simply put, if you look for the good in someone, you will find it, but if you look for the bad, you will discover it as well. It is a choice we all make before we even interact with people in our everyday lives. Be careful with this technique, though, because you can easily find yourself in a position where a manipulator recognizes your attempts to control your emotions in this way and use it to their advantage against you. In this case, you need to take an approach of "hope for the best but expect the worst" mentality. This is done by looking for the best in people during an interaction but not giving away trust or committing to anything in the interaction. The best way to defend against deception is with honesty when interacting with people. If you are honest, you will not have anything to hide and will not be burdened with having to remember a lie in an attempt to deceive. More often than not, people will respond in a positive manner when you are honest with them—and this will translate into a positive and desired emotional state.

At the core root of every emotion is the stimulus of thought. Our minds work so fast that many thoughts happen before we can even recognize them as having stimulated our emotional state. When you learn to control your thoughts, you become a master of your own mind and your emotions. The question is, how do we accomplish the goal of controlling our very own thoughts? Many of our thoughts are a result of external stimulus, and as such, we must block out these forces. In some cultures, this is done through Meditation incorporating the use of chanting and audio stimuli, the sound of a calm stream, or a beautiful piece of music. Music is commonly used to manipulate our emotional state in Media and advertisements. The right use of music during a movie or entertainment stream can stimulate the desired emotion at the choosing of the director. Much in the same way, we can use music to create an emotional response within us or accentuate an already existing emotion. This is common among athletes and other fighters before the competition. Boxers and MMA fighters will use music to pump themselves up and attempt to use it to psyche out their opponent. Many people that work out will have a song or playlist that drives their emotional state to an aggressive place to increase their physical output. From Meditation to intimidation, music is a powerful tool used to control emotions. Another tool in controlling the thoughts that stimulate an emotion is to replace negative thoughts with positive thoughts. When a negative thought creeps into your head instead of accepting it and holding on to it, you must let it go and replace it with another thought to occupy your mind. This new thought will be the new trigger for your emotions once accepted. It can be a difficult process to extract these negative thoughts and fill your mind with positivity. This requires effort and diligence and may need to be done in the form of chanting, as with meditation. Repeating a positive thought over and over has power and will fight off the negativity that you are holding onto. With practice, this will become easier—although it will be quite difficult in the beginning. Following these steps will help you to control your thoughts and emotions and become a master of your own mind.

Conclusion

Thank you for making it all the way through to the end of *Dark Psychology Secrets*! It was not an easy read and required a college-graduate level of reading comprehension. Congratulations! We sincerely hope it was informative and as much fun to read as it was to write. Be careful when using the tools provided within, and we hope that you use them to make your life better and to achieve your goals—whatever they may be.

After reading this book, if you find that you are in an abusive relationship with someone using dark psychological secrets and techniques on you, seek out professional help. There are many resources available to you, and all it takes is a quick search on the internet. You no longer need to accept being the victim of manipulation.

If you are interested in learning more about this subject matter, there is a wealth of information for you to research online. Good luck in your journey, and we hope Dark Psychological Secrets has helped you to see the bigger picture of the world you live in, as well as how the techniques described in this book affect our everyday lives.

www.ingramcontent.com/pod-product-compliance
Lightning Source LLC
Chambersburg PA
CBHW061809250726
48657CB00001B/352